Dancing Within The Vortex:

TAKING THE QUANTUM LEAP ON THE SPIRITUAL JOURNEY

BEYOND TIME AND SPACE

Phyllis L. Swenson

Saint Louis, Missouri

DANCING WITHIN THE VORTEX:

TAKING THE QUANTUM LEAP ON THE SPIRITUAL JOURNEY

BEYOND TIME AND SPACE

Phyllis L. Swenson

Dancing Within The Vortex

Copyright © 2007 by Phyllis L. Swenson

All rights reserved. This book, or parts thereof, may not be reproduced in any form without written permission of the author except for the inclusion of brief quotations in a review.

Published by:
    Femme Osage Publishing
    1301 Colby Drive
    Saint Peters, Missouri, USA 63376
    FemmeOsagePublishing.com
    Publisher@FemmeOsagePublishing.com

Printed in the United States of America

ISBN: 978-1-934509-13-5

Library of Congress Control Number: 2007940460

First Printing 2007

Author Contact:
    Phyllis L. Swenson
    plswenson@cox.net

Cover Design by:
    Sarah Van Male
    cyanotype.com

Advance Praise For...
Dancing Within The Vortex

    In reading "Dancing Within the Vortex" you can clearly see how angels hold Phyllis in their heart, and bring her the courage to share her story with the world. Following her inner guidance, and trusting in the world unseen, Phyllis bravely navigated the destiny of her life. She now shares her journey to help you do the same. Discover the stepping stones of her life's spiritual journey, from being escorted by guardian angels as a child, to seeing benevolent UFO's, to indoctrination into the mysteries of the ancient Rosicrucian Order, and ultimately to the meeting of her soulmate. But this is just setting the stage for the soul drama, heralded by a visit from her guardian angel, that unfolds. It is a story of divine romance that transcends the boundaries of human incarnation and proves that the power of love transcends mortality.

                        Stevan J. Thayer, Author
                        Interview With an Angel

    We all have friends we've known for years, who have inspired us with their ability to see and feel beyond what the average person can see and feel. Phyllis Swenson shared the amazing stories that are in this book with me as she experienced them over the years. I admire her resolve to share them now with the world. Hers is a courageous and inspiring spiritual journey.

                        Reverend Dee Swinney, Minister
                        Unity Church in Alexandria, VA

A wonderful memoir of an African-American woman's quest to discover her Spiritual Self and the meaning of life. Phyllis takes the reader through her experiences as a young girl struggling with her self-worth within a Catholic school system, to the loss of her beloved husband and soulmate, Warren, and finally through her ultimate spiritual quest to discover her destiny as a powerful creator of her own reality. Her faith, strength, and knowledge grows throughout her life. A deeply inspiring book.
      Wayne Dennis
      Air Traffic Control Specialist

Phyllis Swenson has had the most magical and mystical life. Her life experiences, along with many years of metaphysical studies, have given her a very deep understanding of the Law of Attraction and faith in the Universe. Following her spiritual journey through life is an exciting example of our unlimited potential by allowing the connection with God. I thoroughly enjoyed reading about her life and her magnificent manifestations. If you are on a spiritual path and enjoy the metaphysical, you will find Phyllis' book fascinating.
      Bryan E. DeLay
      Commercial Real Estate Agent

I have known Phyllis for over 15 years. From the moment I met her there was joy and light all around her. She has always been on the spiritual path and I've seen her journey change and deepen over the years. Phyllis writes and shares in a down-to-earth, everyday reality that everyone can relate to and see the parallel meanings in their own lives. One of her most important messages is: Don't look to others for your divinity, for your empowerment, for your joy, for your light. Make your journey an inside job, not outside, and find the treasure of the Universe and all you can possibly want to feel and be inside yourself. The beauty of this message is that once you do that, you'll realize how vast the outside help and support is from the Spiritual realms, as well as friends and family.

                Ruth M. Van Landingham, Owner
                Terra Christa Metaphysical
                Marketplace
                Vienna, VA

This work provides a fascinating glimpse into the spiritual life of a modern African-American woman. It reinforces the belief that there are positive forces helping us through life's journey. An exciting and inspirational read.

                Fred Sitzler
                Licensed Professional Counselor

Phyllis' spiritual journey is inspirational on many levels. Her creative and fascinating book allows the reader to experience her personal quest of self-discovery. The reader is transformed as they feel her grow and change and overcome obstacles. Phyllis has an enthusiasm and zest for life that resonates in her writer's voice. She is a compassionate and caring individual...a guardian angel to all those she touches.

                Jane Delpopolo
                Psychotherapist and Career
                Counselor

In Loving Memory of
Warren H. Swenson
(1950 – 1994)

Dedicated to
Bryan E. DeLay
And
Wayne John Dennis

Acknowledgements

I wish to express my sincere appreciation to all of the wonderful people who encouraged me to write this book and whose faith in me made it all possible: The dedicated staff and co-workers at The Women's Center of Northern Virginia, especially Donna Hager, Gale Gearhart, Fred Sitzler, Cathy Love, Jane Delpopolo and Donna Brand; my friends Bryan E. Delay, Wayne John Dennis, Brent Gudmundson, James Carr, Roy Stephens, Brenda Pierce, Charlie Balogh, Ruth Van Landingham, Claudia and Bill Decicco and Reverend Dee Swinney, Minister of Unity Church in Alexandria, VA; my mentor and motivational coach, Marc Allen, President of New World Library Publishers.

I also wish to thank Lynne Klippel, President and Chief Operating Officer of Femme Osage Publishing, whose encouragement, advice and valued support in assisting me with the publication of this book is deeply appreciated. All of you have blessed my life with joy and I am eternally grateful.

Table Of Contents

Preface: The 10 Empowerments	11
Introduction	13
Poem: A Distant Dreamer	19
Poem: An Idea	20
Chapter 1: Guardian Angel	21
Poem: Synchrony	24
Chapter 2: Extraterrestrial Encounter	27
Poem: Prayer To The Dawn	31
Chapter 3: The Magical Turtle	33
Poem: As Above, So Below	36
Poem: Living Stage	37
Chapter 4: Channeled Writing	39
Poem: Child Of Light	46
Poem: Humility	47
Poem: Life Force	48
Chapter 5: Breakdown To Breakthrough: Transcending Chemical Addiction	49
Poem: Mystery	53
Chapter 6: "There's Your Husband"	55
Poem: For You, My Love	58
Chapter 7: I, The Ultimate Observer	61
Poem: Vision	63
Poem: Divinity	64
Chapter 8: The Sound Of Silence	65
Poem: Power	68
Chapter 9: Angelic Leprechaun	69
Poem: Transformation	71
Poem: Smile	72
Chapter 10: Dancing In The Clouds	73
Poem: Rebirth	76

Chapter 11: Manifesting A Thunderstorm	77
Poem: Celestial Music	83
Chapter 12: Music Of The Spheres	85
Poem: Lotus	87
Poem: Solitude	88
Chapter 13: Into The Light - The Death Of My Beloved	89
Poem: Treasure Of My Heart	99
Chapter 14: A Gift From Heaven	101
Poem: Celestial Garden Of Light	105
Chapter 15: A Channeled Message	107
Poem: Song Of Praise	110
Chapter 16: Merkabah, Star Of Light	111
Poem: Remember	116
Chapter 17: A Most Unusual Halloween	119
Poem: God's Calling	124
Chapter 18: My Intergalactic Friend	127
Poem: Celestial Temple	133
Chapter 19: Activating The Star Seed	135
Poem: Christ, The Mirror Within	138
Conclusion: Follow Your Bliss	141
Poem: Ascension	145
About The Author	147

Preface

The 10 Empowerments

1. I AM the Divine Source of Freedom. You are empowered with the freedom to seek Me, your Higher Self above all else.

2. Love all life and all creatures great and small as you love yourself.

3. Live to express joy in life and in all that you do, for you are blessed.

4. Feel appreciation and goodness within your heart for all life, all of nature, all people and for all your abundance. Abundance is your birthright.

5. Know that you are a powerful Being and that your power flows from the Source of Universal Energy.

6. Keep alive all knowledge, wisdom and guidance from within, for you are whole and complete.

7. Devote yourself each day to delicious moments of passion and experiencing life deeply and richly.

8. Know your worth, live each moment with enthusiasm and experience it as a wonderful delight that enlivens, enriches and empowers your soul.

9. In all things, think, feel, and be positive. Know that the Universe loves you with an everlasting love.

10. Bless all of life, know that all is well, be optimistic, and always hope for the best for the best is within you. There is great love, eternal joy, absolute freedom, Divine power, and Universal abundance within you to create the wonderful life that you deserve.

Introduction

There is a popular and inspirational story about a three-year old girl whose parents arrived home from the hospital with their newborn son. Their daughter insisted on spending time alone in the nursery with her little brother. The parents allowed this, while listening in over the intercom. The little girl walked into the room and approached the crib. As she gazed into the eyes of her little brother, so tiny and so new in the world, there was a moment of silence. Then, the amazed parents heard these precious words spoken out of the mouth of their daughter to her little brother: "Baby, remind me what God is like. I am beginning to forget."

What an amazing story. How wise this little girl was to recognize the fact that she was beginning to lose sight of a Greater Power within herself and know that the same Great Power was still present within the eyes of her newborn brother. That little girl's story is our story. Haven't we, in this material world of illusory images, daily stresses, constant headlines of war, destruction, poverty, violence and social chaos, forgotten who we truly are? Don't we need to be reminded over and over again what God is like?

Like the little girl who gazed into the eyes of her infant brother, we need to gaze into our own eyes and behold the beauty, love, abundance, compassion, truth, glory, and power within us and see the image of God reflecting back upon us.

As a little African-American girl growing up in St. Louis, Missouri in the 1950's, my life was filled with many false ideas and negative images society taught me about myself. I felt like I was anything but a child of God and I certainly didn't feel worthy to be blessed by a Higher Power and allow the creative energy of the Universe to flow through me.

I was told that I was weak because I was female. I was told that I was inferior because I was black. I was told by the Catholic Church, which I attended, that I was born in sin and nothing but dust and to dust I would return. I was not told that I am a strong, talented, and creative little girl with the potential to become a great woman.

I was not told that I am a wonderful person equal with people all over the world; that I am blessed with God-given gifts of creative expression that will bring value and goodness to the world. I was not told that I am an eternal Being made out of, what the late astronomer, Dr. Carl Sagan called, "star stuff."

I was a little girl who got lost, like everyone else, in a world that did not value me as both a human being and a Divine Being. I became hypnotized by the values, opinions, and images society taught me I was. I was a little girl who desperately needed to gaze into my own eyes and behold the truth of my Divine Self.

I got a glimpse of the truth of my Being when, as a little girl, I watched a beautiful and inspiring movie, which taught me about a loving God. "The Next Voice You Hear" was made in 1950. It starred James Whitmore and Nancy Davis (later Reagan). I remember what a positive impact that movie had on my innocent mind. The movie was about an average American family whose lives were changed while listening to the radio. One evening, a strange voice interrupted the daily radio show saying; "This is God. I will be with you for the next few days." I remember the shock and fear I felt when I heard those words. I thought the message from God would be about hell and damnation.

I was in for a pleasant surprise. The movie went on to reveal that, not only did this one family hear the message from God, everyone all over the world heard the same message in his or her own language at exactly the same time. The voice of God broke through technology to reveal His true nature to all mankind. For a week each night the message was about love, peace, forgiveness, harmony, kindness and the brotherhood of mankind.

The message was not about fire and brimstone but about hope, joy, and living lives of abundance for everyone. The movie showed people transformed from being angry, resentful, and bitter about life to being helpful, united and empowered to be the best that they could be, knowing that a Higher Power loves them unconditionally. Infinite Wisdom and Divine Love touched the lives of billions of people all over the world, bringing them a message of Universal love. I've never forgotten that movie and still enjoy watching it today. It was my first glimpse into my own eyes, beholding the joy and truth of being loved for who I am by a Power that is greater than the opinions of the world.

That is what this book is about. It is about self-discovery and self-mastery. It is about gazing into your own eyes and beholding the Divine Source of Universal Power and Love within. It is about going beyond mere positive thinking, which is a step in the right direction, to power vision, which is taking a further step toward a total alignment and deeper connection with Divine Energy. It is about how the Universal Forces interact in our lives in so many ways, enlightening us to how truly wonderful and powerful we are as magnificent creators. Simply stated, it is about being in close partnership with God.

This book is both an autobiography of my spiritual development and a self-discovery, rather than self-help, book. It shares memories of my personal experiences of the miraculous and magical events that manifested in my life as I learned unique ways of becoming in alignment with something Greater than I am. Some of the things that I experienced will seem "out of this world" and, in fact, they are. God moves in mysterious ways and there is no limit to how Creative Energy flows and manifests in our lives.

Positive thinking and changing our consciousness have become very popular today, especially through wonderful films like, "The Secret" and "What the Bleep Do We Know!?" But I also want to show in this book the other side of the coin...the side of Universal Energy and how it inspires and motivates us to live lives beyond positive thinking into power vision. The power is the Power of the Universe, pouring into our mind visions and images of higher worlds and creative energies which lay dormant within our subconscious and in our ability to imagine. It penetrates our minds and aligns with our hearts, bestowing upon us the blessings of carefree living and creative abilities that are magical and miraculous. Life is meant to be fun and joyful and not a struggle.

Jesus Christ demonstrated to us centuries ago that we can do the things that he did and even greater. We have the power to prosper, to heal ourselves, and to bring peace, love, joy, and abundance into the world. Having a thankful and joyful heart in knowing who we truly are as God-like Beings gives us the power to create a world of magic and wonder. Jesus also said that when we become as a little child, we can behold the kingdom of Heaven within ourselves and create it in our world. We are created to live the magic of our dreams.

Finally, in the popular "Star Trek" series and movies, there is a theme running throughout each episode. It is our ability to rise above our programming. In "Star Trek: The Motion Picture," there was a very important question asked by the Voyager 6 space probe which was called "V-Ger." The question was, "Is this all I am? Is there nothing more?" V-Ger wanted to move beyond its programming and discover something more within itself. It willingly joined with a human male and female in order to experience its wholeness and greatness. In this joining, V-Ger, was able to rise above its limitations and give birth to a greater part of itself. It became one with the Universe. V-Ger reached out and touched the face of God within itself.

We too are asking the same questions: Who am I? Why am I here? Is this all I am? Is there nothing more? This book tells my personal journey of asking those questions and discovering that I am more than mere flesh and blood. I am a Spiritual Being in human form, learning from many extraordinary experiences. I am more than the sum of my parts. I am linked to a greater Whole. I am guided in ways that are beyond worldly limitations. Like V-Ger, I too have willingly reached out and taken the hand of something Greater than I am. This is my story. May it be a blessing to all of you to reach within and find the greatness within yourselves.

A Distant Dreamer

Dreams are the seeds of life,
The essence of our Being
Plant them
Nurture them,
Love them,
And you may wake up one day to find
That all of your dreams
Are immersed within the dreams of God.

An Idea

I am a beautiful idea of God
A portrait in Her art gallery,
A thought within Her Omnipotent Mind,
A dream within Her dreams,
Created in Her Image and Likeness
To continue the process of creation,
Within my own mind,
Within my own universe,
Within my own dreams.

Chapter 1

Guardian Angel

The Divine breakthrough began one day after school when I was six years old. It was another typical day at Blessed Sacrament Catholic School. School let out and I was waiting for my dad to come and take me home. I decided to walk next door to the church and wait there. There was a small chapel with a picture of an angel standing on a bridge, watching a little girl and her little brother safely crossing over. She was their Guardian Angel. She was also my Guardian Angel. I loved that picture and would kneel in front of it everyday and say my prayer: "Angel of God, my guardian dear, to whom God's love commits me here. Ever this day, be at my side, to light and guard, to rule and guide. Amen." That was my favorite prayer.

As I knelt there in the silent chapel gazing at the picture, I felt a deep connection with the angel. I felt loved and protected. I knew that nothing would ever harm me as long as I had my angel with me. Life was filled with magic and mystery. The angels and Catholic saints were a valuable part of my young life. I felt deeply connected to the Spirit world and intuitively felt that I came from there and would one day return to my Spiritual family.

The honking of a car horn broke the silence. It was my dad waiting for me outside. I picked up my schoolbooks and walked outside the church. There was something different about me. I felt a presence near me that I could not see with my eyes. As I ran down the church steps, my dad stood next to the car waiting for me. He was looking at something beyond me. He stared into space and I had no idea what he was looking at. I dismissed it and got into the car.

Several days later, my dad shared with me the vision he experienced as he saw me running down the church steps. He told me that, as I was running down the steps, he noticed someone behind me. He said that it was a very tall, shining person with a huge pair of wings. He couldn't take his eyes off this person. He felt deep down inside that what he saw was my Guardian Angel. He was amazed by this remarkable vision. He told me that I would always be protected and guided by this angelic Being; to always remember that I will never be alone in this world. Tears rolled down my eyes when he told me this story. To this very day I am grateful that my dad shared his vision with me.

That was the first experience I can remember of my personal glimpse into a higher world of angelic Beings. What I felt as a presence surrounding me, my dad actually witnessed as my Guardian Angel. Who was this angelic Being? Was she truly my Guardian Angel? I'd like to think so. Or, was she a manifestation of my own mind formed by my intense focus on the picture in the chapel and my fervent prayer to my Guardian Angel? Did I somehow tap into a Higher Power within my own mind and manifest a heavenly image of love and protection in the form of an angel into the physical world?

I believe that there are many different ways of looking at this phenomenon and all of these viewpoints can be true. That event was the beginning of a series of events which demonstrated my innate ability to align with and access the Universal Creative Power within my consciousness which goes beyond the boundaries of this physical world. The Creative Power is both immanent and transcendent, flowing within and beyond my physical being. My dad was able to catch a glimpse of it when he momentarily tapped into a Greater part of himself. An unusual life was beginning for me. The stage was set to reveal to me just how powerful and creative I really am. It was a remarkable revelation, giving me access to the knowledge that I am not alone in this vast universe.

The truth is - none of us is alone in the world. There are Higher Forces in this Universe that reveal themselves to us daily. All we have to do is open our eyes and look both without and within. To see the beauty within us is to see the beauty in our world. We are powerful co-creators with Divine Energy and joy and abundance are our birthright. Our thoughts and feelings are constantly manifested in the world according to our level of conscious development.

New Thought teaches us that our thoughts are prayers. Our lives are precious and holy. What a joy and a wonder it is to connect with Universal holiness and allow the Divine inflow of Spirit to join with us as one powerful, creative Source. We are the essence of God-energy. We are magnificent creators. We are unique and incredible Beings. Align with that energy through meditation, dance, prayer, music, fulfilling work, nature, laughter, tantric sex, or any way you wish and watch the magic happen!

SYNCHRONY

Stop...Look...Listen...
Can you feel it?
Do you sense something new?
Something vibrant?
All around us the symphony of life
Dances in harmony to the mystical beat of
Cosmic illumination.
The music of the spheres vibrates,
Pulsates
And
Regulates order within an ever changing,
Ever expanding universe.
All of us are a part of that change
As we partake in the mystical dance
And move to the rhythm of
Synchrony.
We are the creators of our universe
And together,
With the Infinite Oneness,
We magnificently create with the power
Of our mind.
Thoughts are the music of life,
The very essence of Cosmic vibration.
Our thoughts contain the power to create

Whatever we wish and vibrate to.
What do we wish to create at this moment?
What are our thoughts in the Eternal Now?
Go within and know that thoughts are powerful
And connect us to our reality.
Our thoughts are one.
Let us allow our Higher Minds to manifest
Peace,
Love,
Joy,
Abundance
And change the stream of events.
Let's dance together, hand in hand, with the Cosmos
And create life and energy
That reflects the Universe within
The beating Heart of Synchrony.

26 – Dancing Within The Vortex

Chapter 2

Extraterrestrial Encounter

It came out of nowhere - a bright light in the sky flying at an incredible speed. I sat on my front porch watching it in amazement. What was it? I was seven years old at the time. The year was 1960. At first, I thought it was a comet or meteor. But it began to slow down as it approached my home. It certainly did not act like a comet. It suddenly stopped and hovered above my house. I could see it clearly. It was an oval-shaped metallic object. As it hovered above me, I felt a strong presence of intelligence emanating from it. I knew deep down inside this was an intelligently controlled space vehicle. What was it all about? Why did it appear to me? I watched it for a moment and felt in communication with it. I became excited and dashed inside to tell my mother.

She ran outside with me to see what the excitement was about but she saw nothing. The object was still there but within a few seconds it disappeared. To this day, my mother continues to enjoy reminding me of the day I ran inside shouting, "Mom, there's a flying saucer above our house."

What was that object which came out of nowhere, penetrating the space above my home and capturing my imagination and lifetime interest in UFO's? What was the purpose behind my encounter with Extraterrestrial Beings? This event was very different from being in contact with a Guardian Angel. I was not afraid. I felt a great energy pouring upon me from this craft and the intelligence within it. But why a UFO? Was it because back in those days we were dazzled by Hollywood movies of beings from outer space?

Those movies captivated me as a child. My favorite was "The Day the Earth Stood Still," which was about a friendly space traveler who came to our world to bring us a message of peace and hope. His name was Klaatu and his message was a warning to human beings not to build weapons in space that would destroy us and intelligent life beyond our Earth. Klaatu came to offer an invitation to join a Galactic Federation of peaceful and loving space travelers and to let go of fear, anger, war, and all the things that divide us as human beings.

How deeply did that movie affect me? Was the hovering craft above my home an Emissary of Light and was I in telepathic communication with it? I felt a deep connection with it that guided me to spend many years researching UFO's and the intelligence behind them. That event inspired me to support the SETI (Search for Extraterrestrial Intelligence) program, which was founded by Dr. Carl Sagan, and to become a member of CSETI (Center for the Study of Extraterrestrial Intelligence) founded by Dr. Steven M. Greer. Both groups are dedicated to understanding the nature of UFO's and ET's, either through technology or through peaceful, telepathic contact.

What really took place that day during that close encounter? I believe that there was a shift in my consciousness that helped me to expand my mind and to understand that there is a world of intergalactic Beings beyond our human understanding; that there are higher dimensions that interact within and beyond our three dimensional level. I believe that there is a vast quantum field of Universal energy that we can tap into and experience in our daily lives.

It reminds me of the monolith in the movie, "2001: A Space Odyssey." It was a higher dimensional tool that helped to transform and evolve mankind into a greater level of consciousness. I also know that, since my encounter, I became more intuitive, had the ability to predict things that later became true and manifested many things by using the power of intention. Did my psychic gifts come from that space vehicle and the Beings within it, or did I always have those gifts lying dormant within myself, ready to be experienced, and the encounter was a symbol to give me a friendly nudge in order to evolve my consciousness?

That unique experience was an awesome revelation to the vastness of who I am. It appeared in my life to lift me up out of a one-dimensional way of seeing the world and to behold a greater world of infinite possibilities. It broke through the barriers of my existence and introduced a wondrous new world of quantum reality and a Cosmic connection within the expansiveness of life. The great Cosmic Principle of Universal Creativity opened my mind to a Source of Universal Intelligence beyond my little self. It helped me to see that there is a Higher Self within me, opening doors to the secrets of the universe. For me, it appeared in the symbol of a "flying saucer." For others, it can be whatever it is they create that has meaning for them to open their minds to their unique creative process.

Universal Source is very imaginative and has no limits in its glorious ways of inspiring us to the wonders of our greatness. We are indeed unlimited Beings of creative power, energy and light. What a magnificent trip life is!

PRAYER TO THE DAWN

O Dawn of Eternity,
Your creations await You.
Descend from the sacred mountain
On winged Pegasus
And light a candle at Delphi
Where the Oracle has prophesied
Your Name.
The Lost Word remains within You
That holds the key to creation.
Sing a song to Helics,
O Dawn of Eternity,
And speak the wisdom of the mystics
Who are born whispering Your Name.
Those with eyes that see,
Will melt into Your sacred Light.
Those with ears that hear,
Will attune with vibrations of Life.
Those with golden hearts,
Will know Love's greatest "Secret."
Your Word has been praised
In songs of silence.
Creation blossoms in magnificent splendor.
Mount upon a lightning bolt,

*O Dawn of Eternity,
And sail across the ocean.
Mighty Poseidon awaits You
To carry You into the Twilight of Illusions,
Where dreams
And dreams within dreams,
Await the Great Awakening.
O Dawn of Eternity,
Your Word is written within our hearts.
Help us heal our illusions and experience
Unconditional Love.
Strengthen the flow of our creative power
And join us as we dance
In tune with "The Balance."
Awaken us,
Touch our souls,
Teach us about Oneness.
All mankind will journey with You
Into "Remembrance"
And experience the Divinity within,
Once again.*

Chapter 3

The Magical Turtle

I was blessed as a child to have had many pets. I had dogs, rabbits, baby chicks, a pony and some little green turtles. I wanted a koala bear but that's where my parents drew the line. But I insisted on having a big brown turtle. I loved my little green turtles but wanted a big brown one. My parents thought I was too little to have a pet like that. Of course, I didn't take "no" very well. I don't know how or why I began to think this way, but I felt as a child that my real parents lived on another planet. I think many children have felt that way. I believed that my true parents lived on the planet Venus and I would spend lots of time in my room talking to them.

One day I told my Venusian parents I wanted a big brown turtle and that my human parents would not get me one. I knew that my Venusian parents would give me what I wanted and believed with all my heart that they would indeed send me the turtle I had envisioned clearly in my mind. The next day, I was playing in my back yard. I looked up and noticed something big and brown making its way toward me. It was, you guessed it, a big brown turtle. Here I was, living in the city of St. Louis, and this huge turtle walks into my backyard. Talk about manifesting! I picked it up and hugged it. I thanked my Venusian parents for sending it. I named the turtle Snappy and joyfully carried it into my home to show my Earth parents what my Venusian parents sent me.

My mother was in the kitchen washing dishes when I ran inside and anxiously presented her with a turtle that was almost as big as my arm. She nearly fainted. After composing herself, she asked me where in the world did I get that turtle? I told her, with wide-eyed innocence, that my parents on Venus gave him to me. She looked at me as if I had two heads. I asked her if I could keep it. She told me to ask my dad. I went to my dad who was sitting in the living room. I excitedly showed him Snappy. He was both shocked and curious. I told him the same thing that I told my mom…my parents from Venus gave it to me. I couldn't understand why he also looked at me as though I had two heads. I asked if I could keep Snappy and he gave me the okay.

I loved Snappy. He was a very special pet. He stayed with me for weeks. When he died, I had a funeral in my backyard and invited my big brother, Nathan, to join me in the burial ceremony. Needless to say that Nathan also looked at me as though I had two heads.

How did Snappy come into my life? Did I really have parents on Venus who sent him to me or did I tap into the vast resources of my mind and create him to be in my life because I wanted him so much? We hear about the Law of Attraction and the Power of Manifestation. Did I create Snappy in my mind and was he attracted to me as well? I believe that in this world, anything is possible. It is possible that I was in telepathic contact with

Higher Beings of another world or another dimension whose love for me sent me the turtle I wanted. It is also possible that I created Snappy in my mind and called him forth through my own powerful energy that is a gift from the Creative Source. The main thing is, I envisioned something clearly in my mind, and it manifested in physical form. That was certainly another reminder of who I am as a powerful creator.

The film, "The Secret," gives many wonderful examples of how to create whatever it is we want. We can use the power of our imagination by clearly forming a picture in our mind of what we desire. We can use a vision board and cut out pictures from magazines. We can set time aside to meditate and enjoy the silence within to make that connection with our Higher Selves. I like using the picture gallery in my computer to visualize my desires. There are as many ways of creating our reality as there are stars in the sky. Life is unlimited. Little children are experts in invoking the creative process through games of make believe. When we become adults, we forget about the magic of life and become too rigid and set in our ways. We think that life is hard and that we have to struggle to get what we want. We've forgotten how to relax, play and have fun.

However, if we allow the child-like wonder inside of us to come out and play, we'd be amazed by how powerful we are in creating anything we want. The Universal quantum forces are always there for us to tap into. Being thankful, joyful and positive will open doors to powerful energies just waiting to align with our deepest desires. Instead of worrying and asking "How," the best way to manifest our dreams is to smile and joyously say, "Wow!"

As Above, So Below

The Word of God,
The Celestial Logos,
Sings into my memory
A flowing crescendo of enlightenment
And wisdom
Cascading into my heart
Reflecting inward,
Surrounding my aura with vibrations of
Colorful rainbows
Caressing my soul with perfect Love,
Releasing energy,
Flowing outward to touch the Mind,
Heart,
And
Soul
Of the Universal I AM.

LIVING STAGE

The Mind of God
Writes into my mind
A masterpiece of creative ideas
That are projected onto the theater
Of my life.
I live and move and experience my being
Within the Divine script of God.
Performed for the benefit
Of my evolving consciousness
And for the evolving consciousness
Of humanity.

38 — Dancing Within The Vortex

Chapter 4

Channeled Writing

I've always been fascinated by the new science of quantum physics, parallel universes, string theory and multi-dimensions. They have opened up doorways to so many infinite possibilities. I'm enthralled by the idea that there are many universes and dimensions existing side by side and interacting with each other, that there are occasional breakthroughs beyond the time-space continuum allowing the observer to experience a world beyond his or her current reality.

As we continue to grow and develop spiritually and make these quantum leaps in consciousness, many more doorways to vast possibilities and communication between ourselves and other sentient life forms will open. These breakthroughs in time, space, and mind, with the exchange of knowledge, creativity, and mutual love between human and intergalactic Beings, enhance our evolutionary progress. These encounters create a vortex of energy that takes us higher into realms of unlimited possibilities.

In 1968 when I was 15 years old, a unique quantum breakthrough occurred in my life. It was a year of many changes in the world. The Vietnam War was ragging on, there were demonstrations for peace and equality, and the heart-breaking assassination of Dr. Martin Luther King, Jr. shocked and grieved our nation and the world.

My personal life was becoming turbulent. I was 15 wanting to be 21. I felt like I was too young to do anything. According to my parents, I was too young to date. According to the Catholic all-girl high school I attended, I was too young to wear makeup. According to society, I was too young to vote. I felt tiny and insignificant. My body was going through hormonal and emotional changes and I could not do anything about it. I was lost in an adult world wanting so much to be more than what I was.

The breakthrough from beyond entered into my life and gave me the gift of knowing how truly powerful, wonderful and significant I really am. It happened shortly after Dr. King's assassination.

The high school I attended was predominately white. There were very few African-American girls. There was always a feeling of unfairness and inequality experienced among the black girls at the school. After the assassination, the tension between the black and white students increased. There were food fights in the cafeteria, verbal abuse and a terrible fistfight between two black and white students. I felt very unhappy that there was so much division at my school. At the same time, I was angered by King's assassination and by the discrimination against me because of the color of my skin. I felt powerless to do anything to make things better.

My feelings of powerlessness changed the week when my class attended a private retreat at a lovely Catholic retreat center. It was located outside of the city and surrounded by beautiful trees, lakes and so much of nature's beauty. I felt like I was in a world of enchantment. I loved that center. It was a large place and we had our own private rooms. I enjoyed running around in the gardens and in the woods and exploring the wonders of nature. It brought a sense of inner peace, well-being, and connection with a deeper part of myself. There were all kinds of activities to enjoy as well as great food to eat.

I felt as though I was in paradise. There was a nun who managed the retreat center, Sister Mary Peace. She was the kindest and gentlest soul I had ever encountered. She treated me like an equal and showed me unconditional love and respect. She was very different from the nuns at my school. She possessed a beauty and inner peace about her that glowed and radiated from within. I truly loved her and felt comfortable sharing my feelings with her despite my shyness.

Sister Mary Peace suggested that we have a talent show. Any of the girls who wanted to participate were invited. I felt too shy to join in. Sister Mary Peace looked at me and asked if I wanted to be a part of the fun and allow my talent to shine. I told her that I had no talents. One of my friends spoke up for me and told her that I was a wonderful writer. I was very embarrassed.

Sister Mary Peace asked me to write something and share it with the group. Because I liked her, I told her that I would. But, deep down inside I was terrified. I had no idea what I would write. I went to my room, sat on my bed and cried. What did I have to say that was important? Who was I, who felt tiny and insignificant, to write anything that would appeal to anyone? I wanted to run away and hide under a rock.

Something extraordinary happened. While sitting on my bed in tears, I suddenly heard a voice call my name, "Phyllis." It was a feminine voice and I thought it was Sister Mary Peace. I looked around but saw no one. I went into the hallway and saw no one there. I returned to my room and sat. I picked up a pen and paper and tried to think of something to write, but nothing came to me. I started to cry again. Once more, a voice from nowhere called my name, "Phyllis." Again, I looked around and saw no one. I went into the hall and this time I shouted, "Did anyone call me?" There was no response.

I entered my room again and wondered if someone was playing a joke on me. I decided that I was not going to participate in the talent show. I was getting ready to leave my room to tell Sister Mary Peace the bad news. Suddenly, that voice called my name again, "Phyllis." This time the voice was louder and sounded like it was in my room. I looked around and felt a presence. A mist covered the room. I was more curious than afraid. I whispered the question, "Who's calling me?"

I heard that same female voice. This time she said, "Pick up your pen and write." I felt compelled to pick up my pen and paper. I began to write, and write and write. It was as if someone had entered my body. The words flowed onto the paper without my knowing what I was writing. I was in a trance. I wrote page after page after page with non-stop speed. I lost track of time and space. I was floating elsewhere while someone else wrote through my body. It was wondrous.

When the writing was completed, I re-connected with my body. The mist lifted and I no longer felt the presence in my room. I read what had been written and was amazed at what I saw. It was a play, but not just an ordinary play. It was something very special. I immediately ran out of my room to find Sister Mary Peace.

When I found her, she was amazed and happy to see my excitement. I showed her what had been written and she took the time to read it. She looked at me with tears in her eyes and said, "Phyllis, this is beautiful. Let's put on the play and have everyone participate." I was overjoyed. The play was very simple. It required a narrator, some music, simple props, and sound effects. To my amazement, the music, props, and sound effects were all available at the retreat center. I had no way of knowing that.

That evening, at the talent show, my play was to be the final event. Sister Mary Peace found the desired music. I remember that one of the songs was, "Bridge over Troubled Water," by Simon and Garfunkel. She also had sound effects of thunder. I was to be the narrator. The light switch did very well for the lightning effect and I stood in another room out of sight from my classmates so that I could operate the record player and use the microphone. All was set.

I was in charge of the actions and movements of the students as I narrated their parts. The play had three scenes: the creation of the world; current world crisis; and a future of peace, love, and harmony among all people. As the narrator, I was the Voice of God. I had my classmates experience the beginning of creation when we were an infant race living in a brand new world. I played music with nature sounds of peaceful waterfalls and birds singing.

I moved to current events and how we turned away from God, becoming destructive creatures. My classmates behaved like savages and pretended to hurt and destroy each other while sound effects of thunder crashed and I hit the light switch to give the effect of lightning.

I shifted the time to the future where mankind learned how to forgive and live in peace. I played "Bridge over Troubled Water" which moved the scene from violence to peace. At the end of the play, all of the students formed a circle and held hands. They looked at each other, feeling love and friendship between them. I played some soft, meditative music. As the Voice of God, I invited the girls to express their newly discovered love for each other in their own special way, to know that they were loved with an everlasting love by the Creator of the Universe. The play was over. Since I was in another room, I had no idea how the other girls performed. I was aware only of my part as narrator.

At the end of the play, Sister Mary Peace entered the room. She had tears in her eyes. I was curious to know what had happened. She looked at me and said, "Phyllis, a miracle has happened. Come and see."

She took me by the hand and we entered the room together. I couldn't believe my eyes. I witnessed a special miracle with a heart filled with joy. All of the girls who participated in the play were crying, praying, or hugging each other. The two black and white students who had the terrible fistfight just days prior to the retreat were hugging each other and crying. They found the meaning of forgiveness. One of the students told me that while they were in the circle at the end of the play and holding hands, they experienced an electrical energy that surged throughout their bodies. It was as though they were struck by gentle lightning. I stood there witnessing a scene of love, tolerance, acceptance, and forgiveness and I cried.

I confessed to Sister Mary Peace how the play was written. I told her about the voice that called my name. I told her that I did not believe that I had written the play but that someone else wrote it through me. She was not surprised. She smiled at me and said, "Phyllis, it does not matter who wrote it. You were there as a willing instrument of God's love and peace. Look at the miracle which has been created." A miracle of love.

Sister Mary Peace kept the play and promised to have it performed at the retreat center every year. Since then, I have lost touch with her but I will always remember her as an angel in my life. The moment that she told me I was a willing instrument of God's love and peace, I felt a strong connection with Mary in the Bible when she accepted the honor of bringing Jesus Christ into the world as his mother. Her words, "Behold the handmaiden of the Lord, be it done unto me according to Thy Word," echoed in my mind. I felt that the Word of God flowed into me and manifested into form as a play, which brought into our retreat center a wonderful miracle of love.

Who was that soft, feminine voice that whispered my name, starting a chain of events that led to the healing of anger, racial prejudice, and separation? Some religious people may describe the voice as my Guardian Angel. Quantum physics would probably describe it as a parallel world breaking through time, space, and mind where contact with another life form had occurred. Both are right. It was an experience I'll always remember and treasure in my heart. It lifted me up from feeling like a tiny, insignificant nothing to being a co-creator with the Infinite Power of the Universe. We are all co-creators with God and magnificent channels for the flow of love and peace in our world.

Child Of Light

I am made of twinkling stars,
Golden sun,
Crystal moon,
And I will shine brightly
For all eternity.

HUMILITY

The virgin snows of winter
Fall softly and gently,
Clothing my body inside a
White velvet cocoon,
Forming and shaping a
Magnificent crystal cathedral;
Radiant,
Glowing,
Towering in the midst of nocturnal serenity.
Humbled before God in prayerful silence.

LIFE FORCE

The Mystical Silver Cord
Connects my infant soul
To the Divine inflow of
My Creator's Heart of Gold.

Chapter 5

Breakdown To Breakthrough: Transcending Chemical Addiction

The spiritual journey has its hazards as well as its joys. My journey took me from my home in St. Louis, Missouri to Washington, DC in 1974. I was 21 years old and living in the Nation's Capitol. I felt like James Stewart's character in the movie, "Mr. Smith Goes to Washington." I was ready to change the world. I was serving in the Air Force and had a great job working at the Pentagon. I dreamed of working there when I was a child and that dream came true. I met many wonderful people and loved my job. Little did I realize that the only world I was going to change in my young ambitious life was my own.

There was a down side to this brave new world. I started hanging out at the discos and meeting people who introduced me to the fast life. Along with this came chemical addiction.

Wanting to be with the "in-crowd," I opened myself up to a world that was very alluring. I had plenty of money, plenty of men, plenty of sex, and plenty of drugs and alcohol. My life became a wild roller-coaster ride, growing more and more out of control. Help, in a form I did not expect, was on its way.

I had much to learn. There was still an innocent child beneath the wild party girl I had become. Somehow, something inside of me must have been screaming for help. I was lost in this fast world and did not know a way out. The parties and chemical addiction intensified over many months.

I began having a very strange recurring nightmare. I dreamed that I was lost inside a long, dark cave trying to find my way out into the light. In the cave, I heard loud screams and frightening laughter. Clawed hands grabbed my body trying to tear me to shreds. I ran through the cave screaming for help but the screams and laughter became louder. Footsteps were chasing me. It was a horrible nightmare that tormented me over and over again.

One day, I met a very wonderful man at the Pentagon. His name was Bill and he was different from the men I met at the discos. He was gentle and soft-spoken. He showed me love and affection.

Bill was a devout Pentecostal and would occasionally take me to his church. I was not into going to church anymore, being a recovering Catholic, but because I liked Bill, I would attend services with him every once in awhile. I continued to party and take drugs and alcohol but Bill did not judge my actions. He accepted me for who I was and allowed me to find my own way.

I finally told Bill about the nightmares. They were getting worse and I was afraid to go to sleep. Bill encouraged me to say a prayer before going to bed and ask for

God's help. At that time, I had become too sophisticated to pray and ask God for anything. I dismissed his suggestion. I could handle it without God's help.

The nightmare returned. At the end of the dream, running away from the claws and the screams, I woke up suddenly. My body was sweating and the room was like an oven. I was half-asleep and half-awake. My body felt paralyzed. I could not move. Though it was night, my room had a deep, reddish glow as if engulfed in flames. At first, I thought my apartment was on fire. I tried to move but couldn't. I was paralyzed. Out of this flaming energy emerged a nightmarish image.

It was a terrifying and familiar figure I had learned about as a child. It appeared to be Satan. His form was recognizable from images I've seen in many books. He had horns, a tail, and fiery red eyes. His body was blood red. He walked toward me. I was very frightened. I could not utter a sound.

As he drew closer, I could see his large, erect penis. I knew if I did not scream, move or do something I would be viciously attacked or I would die. My life was in danger. I was terrified. Suddenly, I found my voice and yelled at the top of my lungs, "God, please help me!"

As quickly as I shouted those words, the apparition disappeared. It was sent back to the hellish world where it belonged. My room returned to normal. I began to cry and called Bill in the middle of the night to tell him what happened. He was glad I found the strength to scream for God's help. He encouraged me to say a prayer of thanksgiving and ask for continued Divine support.

That I did. I also made the decision to stop my chemical addictions. My life changed remarkably. I no longer needed drugs or alcohol. I began attending parties in moderation and the nightmares went away.

But what really happened to me? What was that satanic apparition? Was it chemically induced by my intoxicated mind? Did it surface from a deeper psychological and archetypal level within myself which created this frightening image from childhood fairytales in order to help me transcend my addictions? Was there a Divine Intelligence, which intervened on my behalf, using images of horror from my own subconscious to teach me valuable lessons? Did this Divine Intelligence give me the power and the strength of will to scream for help, allowing me the opportunity to find the power within that was buried inside? Was this another breakthrough from the quantum world of infinite possibilities, showing me a better way to live in the world, free from addictions? Did I create all of this from a mind that was looking for a way out of my addictions?

As I look back upon that time, I am thankful for that experience. It was another example of a powerful alliance with a loving Universe and discovering, in my own unique way, that I am not alone.

There is a Power that is indeed greater than the world. It is a Power that has total unconditional love for everyone in the world. It takes very little effort but great willingness to align oneself with that Power. As the Reverend Martin Luther King, Jr. said, "Take the first step in faith. You don't have to see the whole staircase, just take the first step."

MYSTERY

The silent mist of ancient dreams
Permeates my being,
Washing my nightmares
In visions of crystal sunlight.
Dissolving my fears
With the trumpet blast of peace
And freedom.
The mystic poets, philosophers,
Seers and sages
Dreamed the ancient dream of life, light,
And love,
Dancing into my soul,
Awakening my heart
To my oneness with the Universal
Dreamer of Dreams.

54 – Dancing Within The Vortex

Chapter 6

"There's Your Husband"

It was 1978. I was 25 years old and a member of an international nonsectarian organization known as, "The Rosicrucian Order, Ancient Mystical Order Rosae Crucis" (AMORC). Its purpose is the investigation, study, and practical application of natural and spiritual laws. Its goals are to further the evolution of humanity through the development of the full potential of each individual. Its system of metaphysics, mysticism, psychology, parapsychology, and science, guides its members to live in harmony with the creative, cosmic forces of the universe for the attainment of health, happiness, and peace.

I had finally arrived. I was at home with this organization. The teachings felt good to me. My spiritual path began with my membership with AMORC. This was a dream come true and I was completely devoted to learning, growing, and developing my unlimited potential. Nothing could stop me now. I was on a conscious spiritual journey of my choosing and I loved every minute of it.

I joined the local Rosicrucian Chapter in Washington, DC. As soon as I met the people, I knew that I had found my spiritual home and family. The members were friendly and just as eager to learn as I was. The teachings were wonderful. I learned so much and hungered for more. I began learning how to consciously develop my sixth sense and intuitive abilities through disciplined study. I was on a roll.

Then one day, during one of our Chapter meetings, I saw him. He was standing alone in the corner of the room looking very shy. I had no idea who he was. He seemed a bit lonely. Out of nowhere, a Voice softly whispered to me these words: "There's your husband." I was shocked. The first thought that entered my mind was; "You've got to be kidding. He's not my type."

I looked at him again and he looked at me. There was a feeling of recognition. I later found out who he was. His name was Warren Swenson. He and I joined AMORC about the same time. We both were devoted to the principles of the Order and became very active members. Even though that still, small Voice told me he was to be my husband, I avoided Warren like the plague for several months.

As time went by, I noticed Warren's dedication and commitment to working within the Order as well as his sincere devotion to his spiritual development. Our mutual friends also felt that we were destined to be married. They saw Warren and me as soul mates. We worked together on many committees. After a year, we became friends and started dating.

Chapter 6: There's Your Husband — 57

Four years after we met, and the Voice said to me, "There's your husband," Warren and I were married on June 26, 1982. We had a beautiful church wedding with hundreds of friends and family in attendance. It was like a Cinderella story. Warren was my Prince Charming. Our spiritual journey together was wonderful. My 12 years of marriage to Warren were the best years of my life. We were indeed soul mates.

Warren told me that the moment he first saw me he knew that we had been married many times before in past incarnations. He knew that we were destined to meet again and share a love and a journey that many people only dream of. Our journey together was filled with fun, adventure, challenges and growth. He will always be the greatest treasure of my life.

After 12 wonderful years of marriage, Warren died on December 18, 1994 of a massive heart attack. He was forty-four. I will speak more about that in a later chapter. I am very grateful to that inner Voice that whispered those precious words; "There's your husband." It changed my life in many remarkable ways.

Warren's greatest gift to me was unconditional love. He accepted me totally for the unique person that I am. With him I felt empowered. We were equal partners on the spiritual journey. That Voice of Spirit, which joined us together as soul mates, is another of many examples of Divine intervention shining its light of love to humanity and encouraging us to live lives of joy and abundance. Life is meant to be rich and fulfilling. All we have to do is listen and say "Yes."

For You, My Love

My love, I was born for you.
Born to share in your life,
Your light,
Your joy,
Your wisdom,
Your strength.
To blend all of who you are
With all of who I am.
I was born in love with you.
My ultimate love,
Even the birds sing the love we share together.
Listen to how beautifully they sing our love songs;
Songs of praise,
Songs of joy,
Songs of passion.
Songs to enchant us, my darling.
My intimate love,
Do you notice how softly the wind echoes our love?
I tremble with delight as the wind whispers
Our sweet sounds of love,
Sounds of peace,
Sounds of beauty,
Sounds of dreams,
Sounds to embrace us, my sweet companion.

Nature, with its wondrous magnificence,
Intricate design,
And subtle perfection,
Share with us our innermost secrets.
Life smiles upon our passionate love
And silently blesses the oneness
We share together.
My eternal sweetheart,
I was born to love you.
To share the Master Plan of the Universe
To be one with you in joy and ecstasy.
We share a forever love
And our hearts will embrace eternally.
Let the heavens glorify our love
And together
With the birds,
The wind
And the glory of nature,
We will float upon a cosmic cloud,
Creating rainbows of love across the universe.
Together we will create oceans of enchantment
And sing our love songs across the cosmos.
We will whisper sweet words of praise
And know only love and joy,
Within the cosmic ocean
Of eternal dreams.

60 – Dancing Within The Vortex

Chapter 7

I, The Ultimate Observer

In the wonderful film, "What the Bleep Do We Know?," one of the questions asked is, "Have you ever looked at yourself through the eyes of the Ultimate Observer?" It's a great documentary about quantum physics, infinite possibilities, the power of the mind and multiple realities and dimensions.

When that question was asked in "Bleep," it helped me to recall an incident that occurred a few years after I was married. I was working part-time at an executive search firm in Northern Virginia. As I walked down the office steps, the heel of my shoe caught in the carpet. I fell down the stairs and landed at the bottom.

As soon as I began to fall, I felt a part of me remove itself from my body. I found myself standing at the top of the stairs watching my body fall down the steps and land on the floor. The whole thing seemed to be in slow motion. Standing at the top looking down at my body, there was someone else next to me. It was my Guardian Angel.

I looked at her and then looked at my body below. Suddenly, I returned to my body and immediately felt the impact of the fall. My co-workers rushed to me and called an ambulance. I was not badly hurt. I was just shaken up a bit. But I played along with the drama and enjoyed the ambulance ride with its screaming siren. The doctor found nothing wrong after examining me. Warren met me at the hospital and we had a good laugh about the whole thing.

The question remains, who was the observer that seemed to be me watching me tumble down the steps? Was it my Spiritual Self? Was this like a near-death experience? It all happened so fast. I felt entirely detached from my body and the accident. My Guardian Angel and I exchanged glances and then focused on my body below. I knew my life was not over and I immediately joined the world of the living again.

That was both an empowering and liberating experience. It helped me to understand death and the after death experience, if only for a few seconds. I did not encounter the long tunnel and the Light on the other side, but I did experience a brief state of existence that transcended the physical. The experience confirmed in my mind that there is life beyond this world and I caught a glimpse of it.

The fear of death no longer concerns me because I know that there is no death...only eternal life. We are eternal Beings of light and love. There is so much living to do in this world and beyond. The possibilities are infinite.

VISION

*With Divine vision
Silently observing within my inner eye,
I can see cosmic illumination
And rise above the eye of the storm
Of illusions.
Soaring triumphantly on wings of love,
Gently landing within the protective care
Of the All-Seeing Eye of God.*

DIVINITY

The All-Seeing Eye of God
Shines upon the pyramid of my dreams,
Spreading rays of sunlight into my heart,
Smiling in blessed silence,
Watching me unfold
Into a rose.

Chapter 8

The Sound Of Silence

It was our wedding anniversary. Warren and I met at a popular restaurant in Washington, DC where he would sometimes go with his co-workers for lunch. I had never been there. The atmosphere was teeming with joy, gaiety, music and the loud noise of talking and laughing people. I'd never been to a restaurant that was so lively. Everyone seemed to be having a great time. It was so noisy that the waiter and I had to literally shout to each other. I couldn't hear myself talk, much less hear anyone talking to me.

Still, it was fun to be around fun people. I was very happy because I was celebrating my anniversary with the man of my dreams. When the waiter brought our food, I closed my eyes for a moment and whispered a silent prayer of thanksgiving for my life and my marriage.

During that moment, something unusual happened. I could not hear a sound in the room. The silence was so intense that you could hear a pin drop. Perhaps when I entered into my silent prayer, I was so deeply in tune with Spirit that I was able to tune out the noise that surrounded me.

After my moment of silence, I opened my eyes and the sounds of the restaurant returned to my conscious awareness. I looked at Warren and saw a strange look on his face. I asked him what was wrong and he told me that the moment I closed my eyes (he did not know I was praying) a bright light surrounded me and instantly the restaurant became silent.

I was amazed. I thought that I was the only one aware of the silence around me during my moment of prayer, but Warren also experienced the silence. I told Warren I was deep in prayer when the silence happened and I was very surprised that he also noticed it. It did not appear to either of us that anyone else in the restaurant was affected by the phenomenon. Only Warren and I experienced it.

So, what happened? I can understand my blocking out the noise while being totally immersed and focused in silent prayer. That happens a lot to me during intense prayer and meditation. But why did Warren experience the same thing? Since Warren and I were soul mates and shared a mutual understanding of the Divine powers of the Universe, did Warren and I somehow find ourselves merging with another dimension that took us both out of the noisy restaurant? Did some quantum event, parallel universe or even a super string event break into our reality and lift us up into a vortex of energy onto a higher plane of reality? How exciting that we both shared this intimate experience of blending together into the Silence.

Chapter 8: The Sound of Silence

The movie, "What the Bleep," suggests we learn to become scientists of our own lives, asking the questions about this complex universe and about these strange encounters that awaken us to realize our highest potential. We are the creators of our reality. "The final frontier", as Dr. Fred Alan Wolf says in "The Secret," "is not space, as in Star Trek, but mind." Dr. Wolf also says in "Bleep," that, "the real trick to life is not to be in the know, but to be in the mystery."

POWER

One tiny butterfly freely glides
Across the rainbow
On its journey toward the sun.
As it reaches its destiny,
Its energies burst forth across the cosmos,
Splashing a dazzling array of colors
Across the universe,
Creating a new sun,
New energies,
New life,
New meaning.

Chapter 9

Angelic Leprechaun

Warren and I decided to spend one of our summer vacations in Great Barrington, Massachusetts. We stayed at a charming bed and breakfast. The food was great, the jazz music entertaining, and the room was lovely. We visited the botanical gardens, spent time at the Shaker Village, and shopped at the quaint gift shops. The most fun we had was hiking in the mountains. We often hiked in Shenandoah, in the Blue Ridge Mountains of Virginia, and looked forward to climbing one of the tallest mountains in Great Barrington.

The hike was wonderful. It was a beautiful, sunny summer's day. There was an air of enchantment and mystery surrounding us as we climbed. I felt there were many eyes in the Spirit world watching us. When we reached the top of the mountain and witnessed the breathtaking view of the valley below, we felt like Gods beholding a wondrous world. We sat there for a long time and marveled at the beauty of nature.

It was getting late and we knew we had to leave before it got dark. As we hiked down the mountain, I continued to have that strong feeling of being watched. There were many animals there. Nature was teeming with life. It began to grow dark.

Warren and I lost our way on the trail. We weren't sure if we were heading in the right direction to the parking lot. Finding ourselves lost felt very unsettling. I said a quick prayer to the nature Spirits to help us.

Within minutes, we heard someone walking behind us. We looked around and saw a very tall, very skinny gentleman. He wore a green outfit, funny green hat, and green shoes. He carried a walking stick. I tried to maintain a poker face when I looked at him because he looked very funny in his strange outfit. He reminded me of pictures of leprechaun's I'd seen as a child in story books. Before I could say anything, he spoke to us with a distinct Irish accent and asked us if we were lost. I said yes and he said, "Follow me."

We followed him down the trail trying to keep up because he walked very fast. I thought to myself that this was a very interesting and humorous answer to my prayer to the nature Spirits. It's just like them to send me an angelic leprechaun! Finally, we reached the parking lot. Warren and I saw our car and happily looked at each other. We turned around to thank the man for helping us but he had vanished. I thanked the nature Spirits for sending us such a jolly angel to help us.

Life truly is amazing. The more I experience and understand the Law of Attraction and the loving support of the Universe, the more the vast imagination of the creative process amazes me. How I attracted a person dressed like a leprechaun is beyond my understanding. There was something inside of me that drew him to us to guide us out of the woods. The Universe has a sense of humor and loves for us to enjoy life. Perhaps that is why the quantum world is such a wacky world of miracles, magic, and fun.

Chapter 9: Angelic Leprechaun

TRANSFORMATION

I saw you today
As you graced upon the waters
So cool, so majestic
As the ocean bathed you
With love and joy.
I saw you today
As you glided upon the clouds.
Your eyes filled with beauty
As you melted into the sun.
I saw you today,
Graceful,
Triumphant,
Glorious.
I beheld a miracle today.
Today I saw....
Me!

SMILE

A smile is like a rainbow,
Full of bright colors and cheerfulness.
Go out today and smile at everyone you meet
And you may find
At the end of each rainbow,
A treasure of love,
Happiness,
And
Friendship.

Chapter 10

Dancing In The Clouds

It was a hot summer day. Warren and I were invited to a barbecue in Maryland with many of our Rosicrucian friends. We had a great time socializing with each other. One of our friends, Mary, was a talented poet. We often enjoyed listening to her poetry readings. After lunch, we gathered around Mary to listen to her latest poems. We made ourselves comfortable in lawn chairs. Warren had a chair for me and wanted me to sit next to him. I felt the desire to lie down on the grass away from everyone and enjoy Mother Nature. While everyone sat in their chairs, I laid comfortably on the grass behind them. Mary stood in front of us and read her poetry.

No one could see me but Mary. I was enjoying the sun shining on me and the clouds passing overhead. The clouds were a beautiful white. I looked at them and contemplated their shapes. I became lost in my imagination and felt united with the sky above me. I lifted my arms toward the sky as though I could touch the clouds. I began to breathe deeply and felt the rhythm of the universe. The deeper I breathed, the closer I felt an emergence with the sky and the clouds. Within minutes I felt as though I was being lifted up into the sky.

I felt myself floating in air. I had experienced astral travel on several occasions but this time the experience was more intense. I experienced oneness with the clouds. I reached out and actually touched them. I literally felt myself among the clouds, dancing inside them and feeling an intense connection with the universe. It was such a wonderful experience. I looked down upon Mother Earth and beheld her glorious beauty. How wonderful it was to feel free and uninhibited. How long was I there? There is no time in the universe. There is only the Now. I was a free bird soaring magically beyond time and space.

The poetry reading was over and I gently felt myself return to Earth. Everyone gathered around to congratulate Mary. Warren and I joined the others. When I went with the others to talk to Mary, she pulled me aside to speak to me privately. What she said nearly knocked me off my feet. As she was reading her poems, she saw me lying on the grass. She then noticed me raising my arms toward the sky and, in the blink of an eye, saw my body disappear!

I was amazed. I thought that only my spirit had projected itself into the clouds while my body continued to lie on the grass. But, according to Mary, my physical body actually disappeared! How could that be? Mary couldn't have known that I had felt myself being lifted into the clouds, and I had no idea my body literally disappeared right before her eyes. How amazing that both Mary and I were mutual witnesses to a miraculous experience that defies logic and classical physics as we understand it with our finite minds.

Chapter 10: Dancing In The Clouds

There are stories of Indian yogis who could disappear, walk on water, walk through walls, bi-locate, etc. I know that some very advanced Western mystics have also done those things. The Rosicrucian teachings speak of the ability to form clouds around us so that we can disappear in them. Is that what happened to me? But Mary saw no clouds around me. She only saw my body disappear.

In the quantum world, subatomic particles do strange and wacky things. They can appear as waves and as particles. They can be in two places at one time. They can disappear in one dimension and reappear in another. They do not die and cannot be destroyed. They play in a wild world of endless possibilities.

What happens in the larger world when the mind encounters these quantum critters? Do they create something wholly different and seemingly impossible? What is real and what is illusion? How do you make sense of something beyond human logic when you bump into the quantum world that introduces you to its menagerie of infinite possibilities? Just like the young boy asks in, "What the Bleep," "How far down the rabbit hole do you want to go?", the quantum world challenges us to ask the same question. Like Alice in Wonderland, I can go as far as my imagination takes me. The quantum merry-go-round offers a world of wonder, mystery, joy, and an exciting excursion through the vortex of alternate realities. Want to take a ride down its wild and exciting rabbit hole?

Rebirth

In the dark night of the seventh cycle,
When the moon is full
And the tide rises,
Crashing fiercely upon the crystal shore,
The crimson Phoenix within my soul
Lifts its heavy, ancient wings toward the sky,
Crying to be consumed within the fires of
Eternal life.

Behold…

For out of the ashes will arise
A majestic new creation.
A magnificent being bathed in light,
Sanctified by the breath of love,
Blossoming into total perfection,
Youthful,
Beautiful,
Powerful,
Radiant.
Ready to spread new wings and fly
Into the Golden Dawn
Of a New World.

Chapter II

Manifesting A Thunderstorm

In 1991, Warren and I had been happily married for 9 years. We lived in a Cape Cod style home in Northern Virginia. Even though I loved our home, it was tiny with one bathroom. In June of that year, I woke up one morning with a strong feeling that it was time for Warren and me to move to a bigger home.

I knew the kind of house I wanted to live in. I desired a large room for a library because Warren and I had many books. In our tiny Cape Cod, all our books were on shelves in the dining room. I use to jokingly call it our "food for thought" room! I also wanted a larger kitchen and more than one bathroom. I wanted to live in a quiet neighborhood with lots of trees. I visualized my dream home and felt deep down inside that we were going to get it.

I told Warren the good news. It was time for us to move. He did not agree. He felt that we could not afford a new house. I was not working at the time and we had no savings. The housing market was not good and he was not prepared to go through the expense and stress. I understood his feelings, but I also knew that nothing was impossible. I told him I that I deeply felt that we were going to buy a new home, that the money would be there and that it would all manifest before the year was over. He looked at me as though I had two heads, a very familiar look. But Warren knew that when I was determined to have something, somehow it always manifested. He left it up to me to achieve this incredible goal.

I hired a real estate agent and put our house on the market. She and I did not work well together. She had her ideas, I had my ideas, and neither of us agreed on anything. I was not happy with how slow things were going.

One day, during an open house, another real estate agent walked in with a potential buyer. When I looked at the agent, there was an intuitive feeling that I had known her before in a past lifetime. She had a positive attitude and a very pleasant personality. I asked her to be our agent and let the other one go. Things started moving a little faster and this new agent, Brenda, and I worked very well. Later on, Brenda and I became good friends.

In the meantime, Warren and I went out to look for our new home. The first two that we saw did not appeal to me. When we drove into the neighborhood of the third place, I immediately felt good about it. The neighborhood looked familiar. As soon as we saw the house, I knew it was my dream home. I jumped out of the car and ran inside. It had everything I wanted...a large kitchen, a large room for a library and three bathrooms. Trees surrounded the house and the neighbor-

Chapter II: Manifesting A Thunderstorm – 79

hood was quiet. That was it. I was excited. Even Warren was getting excited, though he was still worried as to where the money was going to come from.

For the next few months, we had many people looking at our tiny Cape Cod but no buyer. One weekend, Warren and I took a trip to Emmitsburg, Maryland to visit the Catholic Shrine of St. Elizabeth Ann Seaton. We would go there every year to rest, hike, and visit the Lourdes grotto next to the shrine. We took jugs to collect fresh spring water from the grotto to bring home. I loved going there and it became a pilgrimage for me.

Warren and I would chat with the nuns and watch the movie about the life of Mother Seaton. I spoke with one of the nuns and told her about trying to sell our home and my frustration with not getting a buyer. She suggested that I find a statue of St. Joseph, bury it in the front yard, and pray for his help in selling our home. St. Joseph is the saint of homes and carpentry. It is an old legend that is dear to the heart of many Catholics.

Before going home we stopped at a local New Age store. I was interested in buying a couple of books. While there, I talked to the owner and mentioned what the nun told me. What a pleasant surprise to discover that she carried some statues of St. Joseph in her store! I bought one and when Warren and I arrived home, I told him that we should perform a ceremony. We'd bury the statue in our front yard and say a prayer asking for St. Joseph's help. Warren, who was not Catholic, thought I had lost all my marbles. However, because he loved me he joined me in the ceremony. We dug a hole, put the statue in, and covered him up. We said a prayer and left everything in the hands of the Universe.

The next day I had an idea. Warren and I had an old swing set in our backyard which was there when we bought the house. I never liked it and, since we had no children, always wanted to get rid of it. It was old and rusty and took away from the beauty and spaciousness the yard. Perhaps if we got rid of that ugly swing set, our home would sell faster. Warren didn't want to because it would cost too much. The structure was set in concrete and he didn't want to deal with the expense. Warren said that whoever bought the house could remove the swing set if they wanted. I disagreed and could not accept "no" for an answer. I was determined to have that swing set removed.

That night, I visualized my backyard looking lovely and spacious and the swing set gone. I did not know how it was going to happen but I knew that once the swing set was removed, our home would sell quickly. I went to sleep with that thought in mind. Late that night I awoke suddenly. There was a terrible storm raging outside. The thunder and lightning were unusually intense and the wind was very strong. I was worried that it was going to turn into a tornado. I looked out the window. Things seemed okay, and I went back to sleep as the storm continued.

The next morning the sun was shining. It was a lovely Sunday. Warren was already up. He ran into the bedroom very excited. I asked him what was up and he had this amazed look on his face. He told me to get out of bed and look at our backyard. I put on my robe and ran behind him to the balcony overlooking the yard.

The scene in front of my eyes shook me to my bones. The first words that came out of my mouth were, "Oh my God." The previous night, as one of the most vicious storms raged, lightning struck our big oak tree.

One of the large branches fell off, struck the swing set, ripped it out of the cement, and knocked the whole thing to the ground. It was an incredible site. The hand of God, along with Mother Nature, picked up the swing set and knocked it over!

Warren knew I wanted that swing set removed and, by golly, it was removed. He looked at me and asked, "What kind of power do you have?" I think he was joking but at the same time he was serious. Warren called the insurance company and they paid for the damages and the clean up. It did not cost us a penny. Talk about the power of visualization!

With our newly spacious yard we sold the house within a month. A young married couple who had no children bought it. They did not need a swing set. We got more money from the sale of our old home which helped us to buy our new dream home.

We had enough money left over to buy new furniture and new carpet. I told Warren in June that we would sell our house and buy our new one before the year was over. By December, despite the terrible housing market, everything was settled. We moved, along with our statue of St. Joseph, in January 1992. Though Warren knew about the power of visualization, he became less skeptical and more of a believer. Warren and I were happy together in our new home.

So, did the statue of St. Joseph help us? It's possible. The legend of St. Joseph, patron saint of houses, is deeply ingrained in the Catholic belief system. Thousands of Catholic believers, over many generations, have invoked St. Joseph to assist them in selling their homes. A strong morphic resonance of faith has energized the fabric of space. This creates a stable system of Divine manifestation when St. Joseph is invoked for assistance. Focused prayer, recited by thousands of people constantly throughout the years, can manifest results that appear to be miraculous.

I believed that focused attention on the idea of St. Joseph's intervention on our behalf had invoked his energy in supporting our efforts to sell our home. The result of that focused energy was amazing. Also, my strong faith that we would sell our home, and my steadfast determination and focused visualization, empowered my own innate energy to create a very astonishing and successful manifestation.

The energy of St. Joseph is very real for those who believe in and love him. That love is the love of the Universe flowing within us and manifesting our desires in whatever form is believable to the individual. A thunderstorm, stirred up by my unconscious mind with the desire for Cosmic support to get rid of a swing set, is a gift from the Universe. It tells us that we have the power within to create whatever we desire, no matter how big or dramatic it is. As stated in the Bible, "If we have faith as small as a mustard seed, we can move mountains."

CELESTIAL MUSIC

The waterfall of music
Flows in harmony throughout the universe,
Vibrating within our souls
As we dance upon an ocean of musical dreams.
The stars chant a Gregorian lullaby,
The moon sleepily whistles
A peaceful tune of praise.
The heartbeat of the sun blends perfectly
As it sings in harmony with the Celestial Chorus.
You and I are wonderfully in tune
With the Cosmic rhythm;
Taking quantum leaps across
The music of the spheres,
Dancing and blending with the orchestra of God,
Serenading harmoniously throughout the universe.

Chapter 12

Music Of The Spheres

The music of the spheres is an ancient idea. Pythagoras, the father of geometry, taught his students in the sixth century BC about the music of the spheres and its healing energies. The astronomer, Johannes Kepler (1571-1630) taught the laws governing planetary motion. He believed that there is a mathematical harmony in the planetary spheres which produces its own music. Each planet carries its own harmonic tune. NASA has discovered with its satellites the truth of Pythagoras and Kepler. There is a mathematical harmony and frequency within every planetary body.

Several years ago, as Warren and I were sleeping, I woke up in the middle of the night to the sound of the most beautiful music I've ever heard. At first, I thought it was one of the neighbors playing loud music, but it was four o'clock in the morning and the neighborhood was quiet. The sound was not coming from outside, but from within my room. I cannot describe it except to say that it is what a host of heavenly orchestral angels would sound like singing in a choir. Just imagine the beauty of Handel's Hallelujah Chorus performed by the angelic hosts. I was mesmerized and enchanted by the glorious music which surrounded me.

A brilliant white light began to shine in my room. It was so bright I thought it would wake up Warren. He remained asleep. Within the light at the foot of my bed, emerged a beautiful Being of Light. I knew this Being to be my Guardian Angel. I smiled and said "Hello." She smiled back at me in all her radiance. Her message to me was simple, "God loves you and sends you the gift of music." She disappeared and the music stopped. There remained a sweet fragrance of roses filling the air in my room. I was so grateful for the visit and for the opportunity to hear the heavenly chorus.

I have watched many episodes of the popular TV show, "Touched by an Angel." Each of the episodes explored human drama and human conflict. But all who were visited by the angels were given one simple message, "God loves you." A loving and supportive Universe constantly blesses us with Emissaries of Light to guide us and remind us that we are not alone and that all is well no matter what our challenges are.

Chapter 12: Music Of The Spheres — 87

LOTUS

The sacred lotus blossom
Reveals to me
The secrets of the ages,
And all that God can see.

SOLITUDE

In the silence of my soul
I die,
To be born again,
By the gentle kiss of God.

Chapter 13

Into The Light

The Death Of My Beloved

All the world's great religions teach us that God is love. New Thought and New Age spirituality, as well as channeled messages, teach us that there are Universal forces that love, guide and support us. The love from this Universal Energy is unconditional. We are created in the image and likeness of the Divine Source and we have free will to choose our reality and our destiny.

The ancient Mystery Schools taught its students about reincarnation and the freedom we have, as souls before birth into our current incarnation, to choose our parents and lifestyle. We have the free will during our lifetime to change our goals and destiny as we evolve in consciousness. We are even free to choose the method and the time of our departure from this world, consciously or unconsciously.

True freedom is the recognition that we are responsible for everything that occurs in our lives through the power of our thoughts, feelings, and choices. No one else can choose our destiny. We choose it ourselves.

Peace will manifest in our world when we discover our true natures as Divine Beings with free will, and the allowance of that same free will in others.

That is what I had to do on December 18, 1994. I had to stand aside and allow my husband, who was my lover and my best friend, to chose, through the power and wisdom of his eternal soul, to make his transition from this world into the Light of God. It was the hardest lesson in life I ever faced. I had to freely let him go with all the love in my heart. It was a challenge that left me devastated and unsure about my relationship with God. Warren's death at a young age left me with many questions and doubts about the unconditional love of a God who is suppose to support my joy in life with many wonderful gifts. My husband was a wonderful gift. So, why was that gift taken away from me?

The events that took place prior to my husband's death were mind-boggling. The Universal love of God came rushing into my life, overwhelming me with its depth and power. It was two weeks before Christmas. Warren and I were members of a local Episcopal Church. The people were friendly and we enjoyed the both the fellowship and the Sunday services.

On that particular Sunday, the priest gave a very good and inspiring sermon about the meaning of Christmas in the lives of each individual. He invited the congregation to spend the week reflecting on the holiday and its meaning in our lives. I thought his suggestion was a great idea and began to ponder the meaning of Christmas in my life.

The month before, during the Thanksgiving holiday, I was very happy and thankful for my life, especially for my wonderful marriage to a man who was the best friend I ever had. I was thankful for my home, my friends, and all of the adventures and experiences in my life, which helped me to become the woman I am today.

However, during the following month I began to feel a shift in my thinking and feeling. I felt an air of doom overshadowing me and I had no idea why I was beginning to feel depressed and fearful.

I decided to write about my feelings. Two days before Warren's death, I wrote a letter to the priest of my church and told him I was experiencing deep feelings of fear and sadness that Christmas season. I remember one line in that letter which read, "Somehow, I feel that my joy is going to be taken away from me."

I had no idea why I felt that way. I showed the letter to Warren before mailing it. After reading it, he asked, "What's going on? Is there something wrong?" I could not answer him with words. I only cried in his arms. Warren assured me that everything was going to be okay. We were going to have a wonderful Christmas together. But even his loving assurance did not remove the fear in my heart. It was Friday, December 16. I mailed the letter to my priest that day.

The next day was a typical Saturday. Warren and I enjoyed the day together and went out to dinner that evening. However, the feelings of fear and sadness continued to haunt my heart and mind. That night while preparing for bed, I told Warren that I did not feel like attending services the next day. I wanted to spend all my time alone with him. He agreed.

That night while my husband and I made love, I experienced his love as though it was brand new. It was as if this was the first time we met and grew in love with each other. His body felt so good inside of mine.

I loved everything about him. His deep voice always sent shivers up and down my spine. His body was tall, slim, and sexy as Adonis in Greek mythology. His smile always brought joy to my heart. His silly jokes made me laugh whether they were funny or not. His wisdom always gave me strength. His encouragement let me know that he believed in me and my creative abilities. His deep blue eyes twinkled with love and admiration for me. They were the windows to his beautiful soul, which looked within my soul, merging us together as one spirit.

As I held my beloved in my arms, smelling the scent of his body and feeling his love pour into me, I felt the intense power of our love. There was a spirit of peace surrounding our bedroom. It was as though the sacredness of heaven blessed us with serenity and bliss. I laid my head on Warren's shoulder, listening to the sounds of his snoring. I kissed his shoulder as he slept. Little did I know this would be the last night I would sleep next to his sensual body. I fell peacefully asleep in the arms of my best beloved one.

The next morning, Sunday, December 18, Warren got up before me. As I lay in bed listening to his footsteps, tears came to my eyes. I was extremely depressed and had no idea why I was crying.

Suddenly, an intense energy surrounded my bedroom. I felt the presence of two Spiritual Beings, one sitting on the edge of my bed and the other standing next to us. The one on the bed began to caress my face. A male voice said to me over and over, "I'm here, I'm here."

The other Being, who was standing, I felt to be my Guardian Angel. The one sitting on my bed radiated a love that was over-powering. I felt this loving Being to be Jesus Christ. The love I felt from Him as He caressed my face poured into my body. The gentle touch of His hand on my cheek and His intense love remained with me as I got out of bed to face my greatest heartache.

After drying my eyes, I walked down the hallway and headed toward the bathroom. It was a bright, beautiful day and the sun was shining through the picture window in our living room. I saw Warren for a few seconds walking from the living room to the kitchen. What I saw sent shivers down my spine.

As Warren walked from one room to the next, there was a black cloud surrounding him. I've never seen anything like it before. "What is that?", I thought. Then Warren walked into the kitchen. I walked into the bathroom and turned on the water faucet. Within seconds, I heard a crash.

Before I could turn off the water, I ran to the kitchen feeling that something was wrong. When I reached the kitchen, there on the floor was my husband. He was having a heart attack. I screamed, rushed toward him, and held him in my arms. I got on the phone and dialed 911.

I screamed over the phone to the operator, asking for help for my husband. He gently calmed me down and gave me instructions to use CPR. I followed his directions and looked for vital signs. I found none. I tried and tried to breathe life back into my husband but he was not responding.

As I screamed and cried and held him in my arms, I noticed his eyes. He was staring at me. Even as the life was leaving his body, his eyes continued to look into mine. Warren was gazing, in the final moments of his physical life, into the face of his wife. He was dying in the arms of the woman he loved...the woman who loved him, nurtured him, bandaged his cut fingers, cooked his meals, made our home into a haven from the outside world, brought him joy, laughter and challenges and gave him the best years of his life. I was the last person he saw from the eyes of his soul.

His eyes stared into me as I held him in my arms. The operator kept talking to me but I no longer heard anything he was saying. I was mesmerized by Warren's gaze. I asked the operator to be silent for a moment. I wanted to talk to my husband. The last words I spoke to Warren were words of love. I said a prayer and told him that he was with God now. "Go into the Light, my darling", were the last words I said to him. With a silent prayer, I kissed my beloved and sent him on his journey. His soul went peacefully from my arms into the arms of God.

The next few days were a foggy blur. I felt as though I was sleepwalking through all the motions of the funeral and all the emotions surrounding it. Family members and dear friends gathered to comfort me and say their final farewells to a man who touched their lives with love and kindness.

I remember talking to the priest about the letter I mailed to him. He received the letter the day before

Warren's death. I asked him what he thought its meaning was. Did I have a premonition of Warren's death and, if so, how did I know? He was just as baffled as I was. His only answer was, "I don't know."

I had to live with that mystery for many years. No matter how much friends and family tried to comfort me, I could not be comforted. My beloved was dead. Why? Why would a loving God take him from me? Why would Warren choose on some level of consciousness to leave me? Why, after just 12 years of marriage to my beloved soul mate were we apart in this way? Did I do something wrong? Was God punishing me? Was I not a good wife? Was Warren angry with me? I felt lost, confused, depressed, angry, and completely alone. Why, why, why? We were so happy together. What went wrong?

No matter how much I tried to use my rational mind to answer these questions, I could find no answers within my heart. I was devastated. I felt betrayed by God, by the Universe and by my husband. I wanted to die. Life had lost its meaning. The heartache of losing Warren, who was given to me as a gift from heaven, was devastating. Why did heaven take him back?

That was the worst Christmas of my life. I spent Christmas Day with some very dear friends but it was not the same as being with Warren. Life held nothing for me. Christmas was a joke and I was not in the mood to celebrate.

I had received some beautiful Christmas gifts from Warren. We use to have fun opening our gifts together. Now, I had to open them alone. One of the gifts Warren gave me was a large painting of the Greek Goddess, Persephone, holding the pomegranate in her hand. It is a famous painting by the Pre-Raphaelite artist, Dante Gabriel Rossetti (1828-1882). I've always loved that painting.

When I was a child, I loved studying Greek Mythology. My favorite book was "Mythology," by Edith Hamilton. I loved the story of Persephone. Her innocence was taken away when Hades abducted her to live with him in the underworld. Her mother, Demeter, Goddess of the harvest and fertility, grieved for her stolen daughter. In her grief, fields lay fallow, plants withered and died. Nothing grew.

Demeter appealed to Persephone's father, Zeus, to rescue their daughter. Zeus gave in to her wishes after her sadness almost destroyed the Earth. Zeus asked Hades to release Persephone but Hades tricked her into eating the seeds of a pomegranate. Because she ate those seeds, she was forced to remain with Hades three months out of the year, one month for each seed eaten. This gives us the winter season. The remaining times of the year, she was free to leave Hades and spend those months with her mother on Earth. Persephone became known as the Goddess of the Underworld.

In Rossetti's painting, you see the pomegranate in her hand and the look of sadness on her face. I felt very much like Persephone when Warren died. I felt like I had been tricked to eat from the pomegranate, that my life was plunged into an eternal hellish abyss. I felt like the Goddess of the Underworld because my world of light had flickered out. I believed I was going to live in an eternal darkness of unhappiness. There was no more joy. I lost Warren, I lost God, and I lost my connection with the Higher Worlds. There was nothing more for me in this world. My life was over. Hell was in my mind and all around me and I felt a coldness and an emptiness with no way out.

However, through the power of God's love to shine the Light into my broken heart, I began to slowly break free from this Dark Night of the Soul. The Light of God revealed to me that I was not alone. I was not abandoned. There was hope. That Christmas, hope came in the form of another gift from Warren. He had given me a video called, "Wings of Desire", as one of my Christmas presents.

I had never seen that movie before. It is a German film about an angel whose name is Damiel. He falls in love with a beautiful Earth woman. She was lonely and desired companionship with someone very special. Damiel saw her from the heavenly realms and desired to be with her and love her. The two of them somehow made a connection with each other on a spiritual level. Damiel decides to fall from the sky in order to love her as a mortal man. When they meet each other, they fall in love and marry.

It's a beautiful, romantic film of love which reaches beyond the boundaries of time and space and reminded me of something that I had completely forgotten. I am not alone. Warren was indeed gone from my life as a physical man, but he was still with me as a Spiritual Being. I see him as my Spirit Guide. I believe that he gave me that romantic video to help guide me during my time of sorrow. Warren knew at some level that it was time for him to leave this world and move on. He was not leaving me...he was passing from one level of existence to another level, but he never left me.

"Wings of Desire," was his loving wake-up call. It let me know that his love for me continues beyond this world and that my life with him was very precious. Our life together is eternal and I have more adventures to share with him on so many levels of consciousness. God gave me the gift of life, which included being blessed with a loving husband for twelve years on Earth. Both God and Warren want me to continue enjoying the gift of life. I am not alone.

My human journey is not over. There is more work for me to do and more adventures designed to uplift my consciousness and bring me much happiness. The Light is still shining within me and desires to radiate into the world. As the Bible tells us, "Do not let your Light hide under a bushel." Let it shine brightly among the stars. We are made of star stuff and the stars within us are born and re-born every day with every experience. Catch a rising star shining within your heart. Let it empower you to create the wonderful life we were all meant to enjoy.

TREASURE OF MY HEART

In the forest of my heart I become lost
While frantically searching for you.
Your gentle voice echoes through my mind,
Calming my fears
And finding me.
Now I know that I am never lost nor alone,
Nor have anything to fear,
Because you are always there
Walking within my heart,
Soothing my mind,
Comforting my soul.
You lovingly wait for me to enter
Our forest of dreams,
To find me...
Once again.

100 – Dancing Within The Vortex

Chapter 14

A Gift From Heaven

The months after Warren's death were very painful. Grief is very personal and everyone experiences it in his or her own way. It seems unavoidable in this world of emotions and personal attachments. I spent hours in deep meditation. I enjoyed sitting in Warren's favorite chair where he use to meditate.

We had turned one of the small bedrooms into a meditation room, with an altar containing statues of Egyptian and Greek deities, candles, incense and crystals. There are paintings on the wall of angels and Ascended Beings. We would meditate together or alone. Meditation helped to uplift our spirits, renew our energies, and connect us with the Divine inflow of the Universe.

My meditations after Warren's death left me feeling empty. My home felt like a tomb, devoid of the living Spirit I use to know. There was a coldness and darkness everywhere. I would sit for hours in Warren's chair, just to feel his energies lingering there. I lost track of time and would not be aware that the light of day had transformed into the dark of night. I slept with his sweater next to me so that I could smell his scent. I couldn't sleep without it. How long would I go on like this? When would the nightmare end? How does one bear the emptiness, the coldness, the lifelessness of the Dark Night of the Soul without going completely insane? Where was the help I needed from a loving Universe?

One day, while sitting in that chair, I began to cry and called Warren's name. I wanted him with me. I needed a sign that Warren was near to me and still loved me. My heart was broken and I cried rivers of tears. My grief was too hard to bear and I could not go on any longer with such pain.

The room began to glow with a warm energy. I felt Warren's presence. I knew it was him. As I cried, I felt his hand holding mine. I felt his eyes looking at me. I felt his smile loving me. He was there with me in my room. It was like old times when I use to cry in his arms and he would hold my hand, gaze lovingly and understandingly at me, and allow me to express my sadness. He was doing that once again, but this time from the other side.

When I felt his presence, I stopped crying and whispered, "Warren, are you here?" I heard the soft whisper of his voice, "Yes, my love, I'm here." I began to smile and asked, "Where are you?"

He said something strange. He said, "Turn around and look out the window." Behind the chair is a large picture window. It was a sunny afternoon around one o'clock. It was a weekday and I was home while most people were either at work or out running errands. The neighborhood was quiet. There were no cars driving up and down the street. There was an eerie silence. I turned around and looked out the window.

To my amazement, standing on the grass in my front yard was a beautiful deer. I had never seen a deer in the neighborhood before. I was thrilled. I recalled the many times Warren and I hiked together in the Shenandoah Mountains and encountered the wild deer.

Warren had a gentle nature about him and the deer would sometimes approach him and allow him to pet them. When I saw that deer outside my window on the front lawn, I was overjoyed. I whispered, "Warren is that from you?" I heard a glowing, "Yes."

I ran outside to see the deer up close. I approached it very slowly because I did not want to frighten it. As I walked closer, I looked into its eyes. We stared at each other for a moment as though we were communicating telepathically. There was a spiritual bond between us. I reached out my hand to touch the deer. It allowed me to pet it gently. Magic entered my life for those few precious moments. The deer walked toward my back yard, crossed the neighbor's yard behind me and disappeared among the trees.

I stood there with tears in my eyes. I looked up at the sky and said, "Thank you." Life began to flow back into me with this gift from heaven. Over the years, I began to see more deer in my yard. They became a family to me. But, I'll never forget that first encounter when Warren came to me in the midst of my grief to give me the gift of his love.

The movie, "The Secret," shows how important it is to always be thankful for everything. The speakers in the film suggest the importance of waking up with thoughts of gratitude and going to bed with a thankful heart. It took me awhile to learn to be thankful again after Warren's death.

The Universe wants us to be happy and live a life of abundance. One of the best ways to do that is to cultivate a thankful heart. Nature is teeming with so much wonderful life. The beautiful grace and gentleness of the deer is a reflection of our own gentle and graceful Spirit.

The gifts I received that day of feeling Warren's Spirit and touching the deer in my front yard were manifestations designed to let me know that there is a Universe that cares about me and is loving and supportive to all of us. The message I received from that beautiful deer, from Warren and from God was, "You are dear to us."

Chapter 14: A Gift From Heaven

CELESTIAL GARDEN OF LIGHT

Come, my beloved, and enter my golden stargate
And walk with me in the garden of my spirit.
Here we will meet again and sing together,
Commune together,
Smell the roses together,
And together listen to the birds sing.
This garden is our universe,
Our creation,
Our sanctum,
Our home away from the world of pain and illusion.
It is my gift to you, my beloved one.
You may enter this garden whenever you wish
And open up your heart and soul to me.
Here you will be loved, protected and understood.
Be with me today in this lovely place
And I will love you once again with
My eternal love for you.
Allow me to guide you and support you on your journey,
So that you may enter the world,
As a powerful woman of love and joy,
Whispering our dreams that will awaken
And illuminate the heart of mankind.

106 – Dancing Within The Vortex

Chapter 15

A Channeled Message

Angels and Spirit Guides surround us with love and guide us in the ways of light. The Universe is creative and enjoys giving us the kiss of life and creative expression.

After Warren died, I went on a search to try to reconnect with him through the help of psychics and channelers. During those years of asking questions and searching for answers, my journey took me to many places and people. I had questions about life and death, reincarnation and life after death. I read many books, attended many seminars, and connected with a new network of friends who were searching as I was.

My life had changed dramatically. I was entering a whole new world of wonder and mystery. Life as a young widow was a solitary journey of self-discovery and self-empowerment. I had to live without my partner...and it was frightening. However, around every mysterious corner was another opportunity to be guided by a loving Divine Intelligence.

Many of the psychics and channelers I met were very helpful. They encouraged me to be in the world and dance to the beat of my own music. They channeled messages from other dimensions, telling me that Warren was alive and well on the other side and that he loves me very much. Still, I continued to search for answers and connect with my beloved.

About four years later, I attended a workshop at the local New Age store in Northern Virginia called Terra Christa. The workshop was conducted by the well-known Interfaith Minister and gifted channeler, Stevan Thayer. I was aware of his spiritual gifts because I read his wonderful book, "Interview with an Angel."

Stevan has an active ministry where he developed and teaches a new holistic therapy system called, "Integrated Energy Therapy" (IET). He also has the gift of channeling an angelic guide named Ariel. Through Ariel, Stevan has helped many people to experience the power of physical, emotional, and spiritual healing. I met Stevan and his lovely wife, Carol, at Terra Christa. I admired his work and knew in my heart that his gifts would help me to continue to heal my grief.

The workshop was very relaxed with a small group of people gathered around in a circle and eager to experience this special event. Stevan introduced himself and talked about his relationship with angel Ariel and about his healing methods. He began to channel by going into a trance and allowing Ariel to speak through him.

Many beautiful words of love and joy flowed from Stevan's lips. The messages he channeled for everyone in the group were received with happiness. Ariel, speaking through Stevan, told me that Warren was standing there next to her. Ariel conveyed a message from Warren to me telling me things that only Warren and I knew.

Warren transmitted to Ariel that he was proud of my achievements over the years, especially my decision to go back to school and get my Masters Degree. I had not mentioned that to anyone, especially Stevan. Warren went on to tell me that he loved me and that he missed the love we shared together while he was alive on Earth. Then Stevan began to cry. It was as though Warren was crying through him. As the tears flowed from his eyes, I too began to cry. The others cried as well. Love filled the room with magnificent energy.

It was a very intense experience and everyone benefited from it. I was absolutely intrigued. When the session was over, I thanked Stevan for being such a wonderful channel and helping me to further heal from my grief. He gave me the knowledge and the evidence that Warren truly continues to live.

Since that time, I no longer felt the need to go to psychics and channelers in search of answers about life on the other side. I began to find joy and peace within myself. Angel Ariel has been dear to my heart since that evening at Terra Christa. I have a beautiful painting of her that I bought from Stevan. It hangs in my meditation room reminding me each day that I am loved and guided by the Universe.

I learned to laugh more since that encounter and release my grief. Laughter is indeed the singing of the angels. As the writer G.K. Chesterton once said, "Angels fly because they take themselves lightly." Love, joy, and laughter give us the wings of angels. Let us fly.

Song Of Praise

When the Voice of God speaks silently
Within the chambers of my heart,
Simplicity echoes in return
Chanting, "We can never part."
When the Voice of God melts softly
Into the sacredness of my soul,
The Light within me radiates
Singing, "Love is my only goal."
When the Voice of God flows gently
Upon the tapestry of my mind,
The Universe within me dances
Echoing, "God is good, gracious and kind."
When the Voice of God sings sweetly
Throughout the vastness of my being,
My mind, body and spirit turn inward
Praising God as, "My Life, My Love and my King."

Chapter 16

Merkabah, Star Of Light

Back in 1988, Warren and I attended an annual New Age festival in Washington, DC called the Heart to Heart Festival. We attended it every year but this one was very special. We met many psychics and channelers who set up their booths and gave readings to the hundreds of people there.

One psychic caught my eye. She was an artist who painted soul portraits. I'd never had my soul portrait done. Warren and I sat down with her and received individual readings as she painted.

She painted me as both male and female facing each other. Above the male and female was a golden sun shining its rays. The female's pineal gland, or the Third Eye, was blue. The male's throat chakra was a purple color. Between them was a bridge connecting their yin-yang energies.

The psychic, whose name was Barbara Love, explained to me that my soul had developed to a degree where my female and male energies were in perfect balance. The bridge was symbolic of that unity. The Third Eye on my feminine side indicated my gift of intuition and development of my sixth sense. The throat chakra of my masculine side was very developed as I learn to find my own voice to speak from a sense of empowerment. The golden sun shining its rays was symbolic of my higher consciousness. I was very pleased with my soul portrait and the message behind it.

Then it was Warren's turn. Barbara looked at him for a moment. She kept staring at him and seemed lost in thought. She said something strange that I have never forgotten.

She told Warren that he really should not be on Earth. She said that he was an angel who left the angelic realms to be with me. He was suppose to be my Guardian Angel but chose to be my husband instead. I was shocked. She then said something that really shook me. She warned Warren to be very careful of his thoughts and not become too caught up in the physical world because it would take his life away at a young age if he did.

My heart sank. I had no idea what her warnings were about. I was not expecting this kind of reading. I held Warren's hand, wanting to protect him. Barbara began to paint his soul portrait. What she painted was extraordinary. She said that she could not paint a human figure of him. Instead, she painted his soul as a blue diamond-shaped vehicle of light.

It was similar to the Star Tetrahedron or the Merkabah, an inter-dimensional vehicle consisting of two equally sized, interlocked tetrahedra or pyramids. One tetrahedron points up and the other points down. It is also known as the three dimensional Star of David.

Chapter 16: Merkabah, Star Of Light

Researcher and writer, Drunvalo Melchizedek, teaches about this Star Tetrahedron in his "Flower of Life" seminars. You can also find this symbol in many books on Sacred Geometry.

When Barbara finished painting Warren's soul portrait, I looked at him with eyes of wonder. Was he really my Guardian Angel? Did he truly leave the angelic realms just to be with me? I have no idea. The story is extraordinary but truth is sometimes stranger than fiction. I kept those words of Barbara's tucked safely in my heart up to the moment of his death. Warren's soul portrait was cremated with him.

During the first few years after Warren's death, I encountered him many times. He first appeared as he looked while in his physical body. I saw him standing at the top of the stairs when I played my piano. I saw him standing on a street corner or driving the car he once drove. I even experienced him sleeping next to me and snoring. That became very annoying!

Later, as I began to heal from my grief, I'd see Warren as an orb of white light. Many times I walked into a room in my home and caught a glimpse of the beautiful white orb flying around and disappearing. I have seen pictures of orbs inside the Merkabah carrying the figure of a human being inside. The Merkabah is an inter-dimensional vehicle which transports an enlightened Being from one dimension to another. When I first saw the orb of light, I began to wonder if that was Warren in his ascended body of light. I got my answer in a very remarkable way.

One night, while lying in bed, my darkened room began to glow bright white. I looked up at the ceiling and saw a very large orb of light hovering there. The orb descended and moved toward me. I was not prepared for this encounter and had no idea what was going to happen. When the orb was halfway to me, I shouted, "No."

It stopped, hovered for a moment, and moved back toward the ceiling. The light began to rotate and turn different colors. When it turned a beautiful pink I began to smile. The loving energy from the pink color warmed the room. I was happy and knew that the orb was indeed Warren's energy body of light.

I said, "Yes," and the orb moved slowly toward me. The orb touched my body and surrounded me with a brilliant white light. It penetrated my body. The energy was intense. I felt great love that I never before felt in my body. It was as though Warren was making love to me in his spiritual body. Loving and powerful energy overcame me. The experience lasted only a moment but the love that poured out from it will last a lifetime. Warren and I had truly become one and a new spiritual starseed was planted within my auric field.

That experience was truly remarkable. It empowered me to grow in strength, love, and joy. I became interested in Sacred Geometry and hungered to know more about the Merkabah. I read books by Drunvalo Melchizedek as well as "The Book of Knowledge: The Keys of Enoch", by James J. Hurtak, Ph.D., which shares in-depth ideas about the Merkabah.

There is an old saying, "In the beginning, God geometrized". The Merkabah is who we are as Ascended Beings of Light. Through the sacredness of sound and the breath, we can consciously transform our physical bodies into Light body energy. We can travel within our minds beyond the limitations of the physical into higher realms of superluminal multi-dimensions beyond space and time. We can do it in our dreams, through meditation and astral travel, at the hour of our deaths, and through the ascension process which Jesus Christ, yogi's and advanced mystics taught us. At that point we make the conscious decision to rise above karma and the cycles of reincarnation and travel the Universe as Beings of Light within the Merkaba, our vehicle into the Cosmos and beyond. A glorious future of endless possibilities and magnificent creativity awaits us with dreams of beautiful worlds beyond our imagination. Life certainly is a magnificent trip through a multi-dimensional kaleidoscope of endless creations.

Remember

In the dark recesses of my sanctum,
A candle burns.
As I gaze into the eye of the flame,
My third eye,
The eye of my Divinely awakened Self,
Opens…Beholding a memory.
I melt into the flame,
Journeying back in time,
A time of the eternal creation.
In the beginning…
God,
In the beginning…
Me.
Together we created an idea,
A thought,
A spark of energy
That exploded into a celestial Garden of Eden.
Some called it the Big Bang.
We called it Love.
I remember how we celebrated our creation,
Dancing across the Universe,
Painting moons,
Hanging up stars,

Chapter 16: Merkabah, Star Of Light

Breathing out galaxies,
As we chanted "The Word" that exploded the whole Cosmos
Into an ocean of Divine beauty.
I recall the fun we had creating life and love.
Yes, I remember.
It seems like such a long time ago.
Yet, what happened yesterday
Is also happening today,
And will continue happening tomorrow.
In so many magical ways.
Creation, like the Universe, is eternal and expansive.
The kiss of life is upon the lips of mankind.
We are beginning to remember and awaken to
The knowledge of the creative power
That lies within and unites us.
We are co-creators with God.
We needn't just reminisce the past and
Be stuck in our illusions.
We are empowered to continue the process of creation now
And always.
The past, present and future are one and complete
Within our Eternal Now.
As the candle flame continues burning in my darkened room.

Reminding me of that first spark of life,
A tear sheds from my inner eye.
I am at peace
Remembering that,
In the beginning...
God,
In the beginning...
Me.

Chapter 17

A Most Unusual Halloween

Time passed and my life changed in many ways. I began to date again six years after Warren's death. Though I met some interesting men, I enjoyed my freedom and independence and did not want to get tied down to anyone in particular. I was busy re-inventing my life and loved my newfound freedom.

I took a job working at The Women's Center of Northern Virginia. It's a non-profit counseling and educational center providing psychological, career, financial and legal services to women and families, regardless of their ability to pay. The Women's Center was very instrumental in helping me through the grieving process. My life was moving in a different direction and I was beginning to feel like a new woman.

Still, something was missing. I hungered for something deeper, richer, and more fulfilling but knew not what. It was October; time to celebrate Halloween. Little did I realize this particular Halloween was going to be celebrated with a guest from beyond this world.

It was a special night. I arrived at Terra Christa around 6:30. I met twenty-five friends and store customers who were just as excited as I was. We were all to arrive before 7:00 that evening or be locked out. I was ready for the event of a lifetime. On this Halloween night, I had decided to take part in a séance.

All twenty-five of us gathered in the upper room. Two gifted mediums were to conduct the séance. If anyone needed to get a drink of water or use the bathroom, we were to take care of those things before seven o'clock or not participate. The séance would not be interrupted for any reason. All of us agreed to the rules. I sat comfortably on the floor, surrounded by a room filled with anticipation. Black curtains covered the windows. The room was completely dark except for one red light standing between the two mediums. It was time to begin.

I sat quietly and reverently. I didn't want to miss a thing. As the mediums introduced themselves and told us what to expect, I became more excited. They went into a trance; the room became very cold. As they summoned the Spirit Guides, I saw sparkles of white light twinkling all around the room.

I then saw images of human forms inside of grey mists flying around and luminous lights flashing everywhere. The room was filled with Spirit energy. It was a bit spooky but I was more intrigued than afraid. When the mediums finally made the connection with the other world, they began to channel the spirits of the dead to each of the twenty-five participants.

It was an amazing experience. Family members, friends, and co-workers who passed to the other side, either recently or many years ago, spoke to each person in the room. One woman was visited by her sister who

Chapter 17: A Most Unusual Halloween – 121

had recently died. Her sister assured her that she was doing well on the other side. She shared things with her sister that were personal and only she recognized.

I was in awe of what was happening and watched the joy on the faces of each of the people. I knew that Warren would appear and speak to me. But I was mistaken. He did not appear. Someone else did. Someone I would never expect. Someone from the very distant past who claimed to have known me in a past incarnation.

When this disincarnate soul appeared and spoke through the medium and introduced himself to me, the hairs on my body stood up. Even though I was disappointed that the soul was not Warren, I was equally shocked and amazed that the person who wanted to talk to me from beyond the grave was none other than Marcus Aurelius, Emperor of Rome (April 26, 121 AD - March 17, 181 AD).

I sat there in awe. Everyone else in the room had been visited by a loved one who had recently died. But I was visited instead by one of the great Emperors of ancient Rome. Why?

After the initial shock, I listened to what the Emperor had to say. He greeted me and told me that we had known each other in a past incarnation when he was Emperor of Rome. He also told me that he is my Spirit Guide and that he has been with me all my life. He knew I enjoyed writing and he wanted me to write a book. He said that when I was ready to write he would be there to guide me. All I had to do was call his name and he would assist me.

I sat there in utter amazement. How did he know about my writing? Was it truly the Spirit of Emperor Marcus Aurelius? No one knew this but I always had a secret admiration for Marcus. I use to read about him in history books and found him fascinating. I have his book, "Meditations," which I've read and loved. He possessed a deep wisdom that was rare among Roman Emperors and I've always felt I had a close spiritual connection with him. With this in mind, it was truly surprising that this great historical figure came out of the blue to speak to me. His words to me felt true in my heart. I felt as though I was reconnecting with an old friend. I thanked him for appearing to me. What an incredible experience.

Now, while writing this book, I feel his guidance and inspiration. His book, "Meditations," expresses many words of wisdom:

"Always think of the universe as one living organism, with a single substance and a single soul; and observe how all things are submitted to the single perceptivity of this one whole, all are moved by its single impulse, and all play their part in the causation of every event that happens. Remark the intricacy of the skein, the complexity of the web."

He also wrote, "It is possible to live on Earth as you mean to live here-after… here I remain, my own master, and none shall hinder me from doing what I choose – and what I choose is to live the life that nature enjoins for a reasonable member of a social community."

He is also quoted as saying, "If you are distressed by anything external, the pain is not due to the thing itself, but to your estimate of it; and this you have the power to revoke at any moment."

Sounds remarkably like today's teachings of creating your own reality, creating heaven right here on

Chapter 17: A Most Unusual Halloween – 123

Earth, taking responsibility for our lives and being in alignment with a loving and living Universe. His words are immortal and his ideas are timeless and true.

It's not everyday that a modern woman is visited by an ancient Roman Emperor. Thank you, Marcus, for your guidance and letting me know that life truly is eternal and fantastic in this world and the next.

God's Calling

Lay still, my beloved,
And relax upon the sacred mountain of dreams
As I call you to be an open channel
Of my Divine Life Force.
Allow Me to enter, my sweet beloved,
And flow through you,
Bestowing upon you My Breath of Love,
Life,
Power,
Radiance,
Energy and
Abundance.
You have answered My Voice,
Accepted the challenge bravely,
And have overcome the fires of illusion
With great success.
You are indeed my beloved daughter,
In whom I am well pleased.
Whatever is Mine is yours.
Whatever is your heart's desire is also My desire.
Whatever is your wish is my wish for you.
You are one with Me,
My life,

Chapter 17: A Most Unusual Halloween

My joy,
My love.
Arise and let us descend from this sacred mountain
And create a new kingdom of heaven on earth,
So that all mankind may experience the love we share
So tenderly,
Together.

Chapter 18
My Intergalactic Friend

Science has come a long way in answering the complex questions of our universe. From Isaac Newton to Albert Einstein, our limited three-dimensional world has burst forth into vast unlimited possibilities. Science fiction of the past, which flowed in the creative minds of H.G. Wells and Jules Verne, became the science fact of today. We have gone to the moon, launched probes into the vastness of space, unlocked the secrets of the atom, created technology that dazzles the mind and explored the possibilities of first contact with intergalactic travelers.

The scientists of today are exploring quantum physics with its vast possibilities within the world of subatomic particles. New theories of parallel universes, string theory, multi-dimensions, and supersymmetry are causing excitement as new vistas of consciousness and creative imagination are explored. Albert Einstein said, "Imagination is everything. It is the preview of life's coming attractions."

More and more people are becoming interested in new science and the development of consciousness as well as the possibility of first contact with Extraterrestrial Beings. Modern films and documentaries, such as "What the Bleep Do We Know!?" "The Secret," "The Phoenix Lights," and "The Elegant Universe," open doors to new possibilities and understanding. They reveal discoveries in quantum physics, the powers of the mind in creating our reality, parallel and multi-dimensional universes that exist side by side with ours, communication with intergalactic and inter-dimensional travelers and the exciting possibility of a peaceful co-existence between human and galactic beings.

The documentary, "The Elegant Universe," was produced by "NOVA" in 2003 and written and hosted by Brian Greene. It discussed both Albert Einstein's Theory of General Relativity and modern String Theory. It sought ways of combining the two theories to form a Unified Theory of Everything. The possibility of not just three but eleven dimensions was explored.

The idea that our universe may be one tiny slice within parallel universes and that multi-dimensional universes beyond space and time as we know it exist side by side with ours boggles the mind. Imagine one day reaching out and entering a parallel universe or another dimension to encounter life forms different from ourselves. What could we learn from them? What could they learn from us? How would such an encounter change our view of reality?

One such encounter changed my view of reality during a cold winter day in January of 2000. My mind reached out beyond the threshold of space and time to

Chapter 18: My Intergalactic Friend

open an intergalactic portal to a whole new world. I experienced a close encounter with a Being who journeyed from his world into mine.

The book, "The Atlantis Connection," by W.T. Samsel, is a fascinating history of ancient Atlantis. The Spirit Guide, Tiagorrah, who once lived on the continent of Atlantis, channeled the information in this remarkable book through Mr. Samsel.

In the chapter, "Opening to Channel," Tiagorrah tells of a special meditation designed to help make contact with the inter-dimensional world of Cosmic Beings. He suggests using one of five crystals during the meditation placed on the Third Eye chakra. The stones were the Herkimer diamond, azurite, lapis, sugilite and fluorite. By placing the stone on the Third Eye chakra and concentrating on it, your consciousness opens up and has the ability to explore and communicate with higher worlds and life forms.

I decided to give it a try. My independent, adventurous nature is not one to follow instructions to the letter. I decided, since I had all five of the crystals suggested by Tiagorrah, I would use all of them. Gathering the stones, I prepared myself for meditation.

I lit candles and burned incense on my altar. I played one of my meditation CD's, "Nada Himalaya," by Deuter. I turned off the lights and placed the stones on different parts of my body. The azurite went on my Third Eye Chakra, the lapis on my heart chakra, the fluorite on my solar plexus chakra and I held the Herkimer diamond and sugilite in each hand. I put on my headphones and an eye pillow to block out any light. I sat back, took a few deep breaths and relaxed. I went into a deep trance.

I began to feel my body vibrate. When that happened, I knew my soul was preparing for astral travel. As my body vibrated, its energies transformed into a floating dance of particles and waves. The feeling of floating beyond the vortex of time and space was sensational.

My body began to dissolve and my soul floated above the ceiling, breaking free toward the universe. I was pure consciousness exploring the vastness of the galactic worlds. The sights and sounds of the celestial bodies and floating galaxies dazzled me. I danced and played among the stars like a little child discovering a new toy. I was free to explore the vastness of the universe and travel wherever I wished.

I traveled back in time and found myself in what appeared to be ancient Egypt. I saw the pyramids and went inside one. Inside the pyramid were many chambers, colorful artwork, and ancient writings on the walls. The beauty and brightness were dazzling to my eyes. I remained there for a few moments exploring an ancient world within a wondrous temple.

I lifted again into the universe in awe of its galactic beauty. Then I found myself back in my meditation room. But the atmosphere felt different. A visitor from another world had followed me back home.

Sitting in my chair with my eye pillow firmly over my eyes, I felt a presence in my room. I saw a bright light that penetrated through the pillow. Though my eyes were closed, I could clearly see my room. Standing before me was a very tall Being of such beauty and magnificence it took my breath away. He, for it appeared to be male, was surrounded by a brilliant white aura.

Chapter 18: My Intergalactic Friend

I can only describe his face as being beautiful. He had black, almond shaped eyes and a small mouth that smiled. He had no hair. His skin was a very light blue.

As he stood before me our minds became one. We communicated telepathically. He reached out his hand toward me. I noticed his very long, slim fingers. He picked up something and held it in his hand. It was oval-shaped and had a brilliant white glow. I remember feeling awed by the beauty of the object and asking what it was. He looked at me and smiled. Within seconds he disappeared.

The room was once again dark. Everything returned to normal. The meditation music ended and I came out of my trance. I removed the eye pillow and headphones and sat for a moment contemplating the experience.

I then began to gather the crystals from my body. They were all there except one. The fluorite that was sitting on my solar plexus had vanished. Where did it go?

My first thought was that it must have rolled onto the floor. I turned on the lights and looked everywhere for it. It was not underneath the chair or other furniture. I searched and searched but could not find it. Where could it have gone? It was one of my favorite crystals. It was a beautiful, flat, oval-shaped purple fluorite.

Then it dawned on me what could have happened. The thought of it made me shiver. During my contact with the Being of Light, he reached down to pick up something. What he held in his hand was beautiful, flat, and oval-shaped. Could it have been my fluorite? But my fluorite was purple and what he held in his hand was a glowing white.

Perhaps it was my fluorite. When I saw it in his hand, I was looking at it from my Third Eye and from another level of consciousness. Perhaps, in the dimension that my visitor inhabited, things from the Earth plane transform into light energy when in contact with a higher world in the hands of a Being of Light. I needed to know what really happened to my fluorite. I went back into meditation to find out.

During my meditation I asked the question, "Whoever you are, please let me know if you have my crystal." Within seconds, I heard a soft and gentle, "Yes."

I asked, "Why did you take it?" The answer came quickly through telepathic contact, "Because you offered it to me and I wanted to prove my reality to you."

Since I've never found that crystal over the years, I will assume that my experience was genuine and that I did indeed have a close encounter with an inter-dimensional Being whose reality is just as real as my own. The division between two universes dissolved and first contact was made with a new friend who is enjoying the gift I offered him.

The universe is a world of magic and miracles. If we open up our hearts to the endless flow of possibilities, new doors of peace, love, joy, abundance and friendship among all beings, both human and galactic, will open up to us, creating a new world of Heaven on Earth.

CELESTIAL TEMPLE

As I raise my consciousness
And enter the Celestial Temple,
I step into the Antechamber
Within the Mind of God,
Beholding the eternal knowledge
Of the Akashic Records.
As I delve into these ancient records
Of Cosmic Consciousness,
It creates within my mind
A system of thought that is glorious
And magnificent.
My consciousness becomes one
With the Mind of God
And the wisdom of the ancients,
As steams of progressive ideas
And vibratory energies
Flow into me from the Celestial Hierarchy.
While blending with the wonders of this energy
I become relaxed,
Self-confident
And powerful.
Always willing to be of service
Toward the upward

*Progressive movement of Life.
My mind becomes saturated with Divine Intelligence
And enchanted with Divine Love.
I am grateful in the knowledge
That I am eternally guided by the love and care of the
Holy Assembly of God.*

Chapter 19

Activating The Star Seed

It's been seven years since my first encounter with my intergalactic friend. There have been times I felt his presence in my home but I never had that same intense contact with him. On January 14, 2007, I saw him again. The encounter was not as dramatic as the first time, but it was very meaningful and it was good to see him.

While meditating with music, headphones, and eye pillow (no crystals this time) I went deeply into trance. I felt my body begin to float and transform into a dance of particles and waves. As my body dissolved from my mind and my soul prepared to astral travel, I felt an odd sensation. I began flying through the universe with a pair of wings! The huge wings formed on my shoulder blades and spread to fly. The sensation was both strange and exhilarating. I felt like the angel, Clarence, in the classic 1946 movie, "It's a Wonderful Life," when he finally got his wings. I soared through the universe on wings of eagles.

When I returned to my meditation room, I saw him again. This time he was not standing apart from me. He appeared to me within my Third Eye. He gazed at me with his beautiful almond-shaped eyes. I stared back. We smiled. He disappeared. A few seconds later, he appeared again in my minds eye. We made eye contact and he vanished. For a third time he appeared and we beheld each other through the windows of our souls. He smiled at me for the last time and vanished.

A flashing burst of light entered my vision. It lit my darkened room with dazzling energy. This brilliant light appeared in my minds eye as a vortex of energy spinning round like a spiral galaxy. The vortex became a wormhole of energy, pulling me deeply into its core. I spiraled round and round inside this intergalactic portal. I felt like I was on a roller coaster ride through space. Another burst of light flashed in front of me. I found myself back in my chair in my meditation room.

What an awesome experience! The intergalactic space ride lasted for a few moments and the energy in my room shifted. I removed my eye pillow and saw my room glowing with tiny sparkles of light. There was a feeling of love and peace surrounding me. Joy and gratitude flowed from my heart for the experience and being re-connected with my intergalactic friend.

This was a profound experience. I believe that my intergalactic friend initiated the flash of light. On a deeper level we had become one. I did not see him outside and separate from me as I did when I first met him seven years ago. This time he appeared within my mind. The bright white aura, which radiated and surrounded him back in the year 2000 was now radiating around me.

Chapter 19: Activating The Star Seed

I intuitively feel that my intergalactic friend appeared this time to activate the starseed that was planted into my auric field years ago by my late husband. When Warren's Spirit made love to me in the form of an orb of light, his loving energy implanted a powerful starseed into the heart of my consciousness. I believe this wondrous experience with my intergalactic friend activated that seed in order to give birth to the knowledge of myself and my true nature as a multi-dimensional Being. I believe that I have been re-programmed to live a life of unlimited greatness and know my Divine potential as a Being of Light and co-creator with Divine Energy. Activating the starseed within me was a wonderful Cosmic initiation that has shifted my consciousness to experience a higher, multi-dimensional level of reality. This activation has proven to me that I am indeed made of star stuff and to the stars I will return.

CHRIST, THE MIRROR WITHIN

Come, my beloved sister,
And sit with Me near the pool of Everlasting Love,
Underneath the canopy of magnificent sunlight.
Gaze deeply into My Eyes
And behold the love I feel for you.
See My Heart beating within your heart
Pumping love and energy into your beautiful soul.
Behold the Light within My Eyes beaming brightly
Into your wonderfully glowing innocent eyes.
As you gaze deeply within Me,
Know that I AM the mirror of your soul,
The reflection of who you really are.
Realize that as you believe in Me,
You believe in your Self
And that whatever I do, you can do the same,
And even greater.
The Christ in Me beholds the Christ in You.
Melt into My Eyes
And immerse yourself into the wonders of
The Higher Self within you.
Let your Light shine and your Power flow
And rise immaculate,
Radiant,

Chapter 19: Activating The Star Seed

Beautiful.
Capture My Eyes into your eyes
And enter the world again as a child of Light,
Beaming a reflection of Our Perfect Light,
Life
And
Love
Into the eyes of mankind.

140 – Dancing Within The Vortex

Conclusion

Follow Your Bliss

Many people remember Bill Moyers interviews with the late mythologist, Joseph Campbell, in the acclaimed PBS series, "The Power of Myth." Campbell was a master storyteller who had the gift of combining ancient and modern myths with psychological development. He expressed the importance of myth making in society. It helps us to understand ourselves, our place in the world and the universe. It was Campbell who made the phrase, "follow your bliss," popular.

How do you follow your bliss in a world that encourages conformity and discourages creative expression? How do you rise above self-limiting beliefs and follow your bliss to create a new mythology of creative expression and unlimited possibilities? How do we, as human beings, follow the example of Jesus Christ who said that "Ye are Gods," and, "These things I do you can do and even greater?" How do we wake up and allow the starseeds within our minds, planted by many great teachers, mystics, saints, scientists, artists, writers, inventors and avatars throughout history, to grow and empower us to live lives of abundance, joy and harmony?

I believe the consciousness in our world is shifting rapidly and has been shifting for at least the last hundred years. Alternative healing, zero-point energy, quantum physics, the Internet, and a growing interest in consciousness development have all manifested within the last century. Now, at the start of the new millennium, what will be the next major leap in consciousness to advance our world into a higher dimension?

I see many signs pointing to a major shift that will inspire us to create Heaven on Earth. There has been a rapid increase in UFO sightings and close encounters with Extraterrestrial Beings. More people are becoming contactees, channeling messages of love, joy, peace, and abundance for all mankind.

Our planet is on the verge of an evolutionary leap in consciousness through our willingness to open ourselves to channel messages and energy from the intergalactic and multi-dimensional worlds. Many people sense there are thirteen dimensions. Advanced Cosmic Beings from higher dimensions telepathically contact more and more humans and inspire them to create a brand new world of peace for all mankind.

These shifts are happening and will increase in frequency as we move closer to the year 2012. The Hopi Indians predicted that in that year the old world of separation, war, and inequality will finally dissolve and a new world of oneness, empowerment, creativity, and abundance for all people will manifest to become our reality.

I see the emergence of a new kind of highly evolved humans populating our world. They are commonly known as Indigos, Crystals, and Star Children. Many of these Star Children began incarnating on Earth within the last hundred years. A significant number were born after World War II and are commonly known as the Baby Boomers. Another major wave of Indigos was born in the 1970's. They are now in their early to mid-30's and ready to take their place in society as world leaders. Indigos continued to be born all the way up to 2000 with increasing psychic abilities and heightened creativity.

The purpose of the Indigos, Crystals, and Star Children is to create a new world and to assist in the evolution of mankind. They bring gifts of healing, creativity, and peace. They are highly sensitive and intuitive and possess extraordinary gifts and talents. Joy and laughter fill them and they know life is meant to be fun and enjoyed. Their psychic powers are well developed and many of them have the amazing ability to communicate telepathically. They are gifts from heaven, here in this world to wake us up and assist us in understanding who we are as powerful Beings of love, light, joy and laughter. They are here to remind us that we are all one. We all have the ability to access our true inner power and potential to create the lives of our dreams. A couple of popular movies about Indigo children have recently been released and are available on DVD: "Indigo" and "The Last Mimzy". Both are fascinating movies about these very special children blessing our world today with hope, joy and love.

We are Spirits living in the material world having human experiences. We are angels playing with life, dressed up in physical bodies. We have the power and potential to be all that we desire to be. It takes vision and courage to create a world of freedom and creativity for everyone. It takes faith in ourselves to take that quantum leap into a world of great potential and endless possibilities. It takes imagination to move beyond positive thinking into power vision and total alignment with the wisdom, magic and abundance of the Universe.

We live in an abundant and loving Universe. The Universe inspires us to be the Divine Beings that we are and live to our full potential. We are made in the image and likeness of Infinite Intelligence. We are Divine potential, experiencing the vastness and wonders of life. We are magnificent creators with the power, wisdom, and capability to mold and shape our destiny. We are an energy field living within a larger Universal field of flowing possibilities.

Gaze into your own eyes, the windows of your soul, and behold the beauty, love, power, glory, and holiness that you really are. See the image of God reflecting back upon you with a smile of unconditional love. Follow your bliss and enjoy the quantum ride in this vast wonderland of magic, miracles, and mystery. Let's dance within the vortex, lifting the veil beyond time and space and encounter wonders beyond imagination.

We are unlimited. We are magnificent creators. We are made of star stuff.

Ascension

When the Eagle lands in Autumn
And the golden sun sets,
The wind will renew its energy
And the sky will open its gates.
Remember this:
You will seek,
Yet never find me
I will transform and melt into forever,
Absorbing Cosmic Consciousness
Ascending
And
Becoming one
With the Infinite.

146 – Dancing Within The Vortex

About The Author

Phyllis Swenson is a writer, poet and teacher. She received her Master's Degree in Parapsychic Science from the American Institute of Holistic Theology. She has taught classes in meditation at Unity Church. She has been writing since the age of four. She wrote plays at the age of 16 and an unpublished novel at the age of 18. While serving in the Air Force, she edited the Air Force newsletter. Many of her poems have been published in poetry anthologies and read over local radio in Washington, DC. Her first book, "Dreams of the Dove of Peace," was published in 1988 under her pen name, Rhiannon. It was a book of poetry and illustrations. Many of those poems are included here. Her poem, "Song of Praise," won a national poetry contest. It was composed into music and sung on the Gospel album, "Hallelujah." She enjoys collecting crystals, rocks and stones. Phyllis resides in Northern Virginia.

www.ingramcontent.com/pod-product-compliance
Lightning Source LLC
Chambersburg PA
CBHW030327080526
44584CB00012B/747